INFORMATION TECHNOLOGY
A Revolutionary Change

INFORMATION TECHNOLOGY
A Revolutionary Change
(In 9 Volumes)

Volume 1
(Digital Opportunities for all)

Editor
RAMESH CHANDRA
Vice-Chancellor, Bundelkhand University, Jhansi (U.P.)

KALPAZ PUBLICATIONS
DELHI–110052

INFORMATION TECHNOLOGY: A REVOLUTIONARY CHANGE

(Information Technology)

Rs. 8000 (Set)
Rs. 900 (Each Volume)

ISBN: 81-7835-201-X (Set)
ISBN: 81-7835-220-6 (Vol. 1)

Published in 2003 in India by
Kalpaz Publications
C–30, Satyawati Nagar
Delhi–110052
E-mail: kalpaz@hotmail.com

Laser Typesetting at: Varsha Graphics, Delhi
Printed at: Mehra Offset Printers, New Delhi

Contents

Preface *ix*

1. **Introduction** **1**
ICT and Education.

2. **Opportunities of Digital Technologies** **25**
Importance of ICT Products.

3. **Development of E-Commerce** **60**
Job Opportunities for Women; E-Business Developments; UNCTAD Survey; Results of the Survey.

4. **M-Commerce Opportunities** **104**
Features of M-Commerce; Immediately; Connectivity; Localisation; Data Portability.

5. **E-Publishing: Challenges in the New Millennium** **127**
Newspapers; Scholarly Journals; Books; Demand for E-Books; Benefits of E-Books; Disadvantages of E-Books; Cost Comparison; E-Publishing in Developing Countries; Copyright Issues; Role of Government.

6. **Digital Trends** **168**
ICTs and Digital Divide.

7. **Challenges of Online Environment** **201**
Privacy on Internet; Legal Protection to Privacy; UNESCO Virtual Forum on INFO Ethics.

Appendix **260**
The Actions; Policy Measures; E-Business Environment; Information Infrastructure; Broadband; Dissemination of Practices; Benchmarketing; Measurement and Analysis; Policy Development; A Co-ordination Mechanism for E-Policies; Financing.

Bibliography 281

Index 283

Preface

The Information and Communication Technology (ICT) is, in many ways, a unique technology. It has the characteristic of a threshold technology, with the ability to rapidly change the whole structure of society and reshape the way our economy is organised. It permeates every aspect of today's societal activity. Ironically, the very factors that have phenomenally improved productivity by intelligent use of the technology, also risk driving the poor to the periphery, thus creating barriers within and between societies, and could lead to social unrest and tension.Countries and people lacking capacity for ICT will be marginalized in the new economy. New trade barriers will be erected. Moreover, without access to ICT, countries will not be able to benefit from the many innovative ways of addressing poverty and basic needs that these technologies offer.

One reason why the information gap is widening is that the potential of ICT in social and economic development has not been fully understood. There are still too many people in key positions in governments and aid agencies who seem to believe that only when basic needs are met does technology have a role to play. If they were right most of the poor would have to wait forever. The debate must move beyond choosing between ICT and other development needs such as health and education. The issue is not about a trade-off between one or the other, but an understanding that these must go hand in hand. However, technology alone is not enough. Technology must be applied within its social context and that, in many countries, is providing a real challenge. One thing is clear. The new technologies, notably ICT, will bring about major transformations in society.

To bridge the digital divide is both a moral and a social imperative. If we do not succeed, entire regions and hundreds of millions of people will be left behind. The consequences in terms of poverty and deprivation will be devastating. New systems of energy supply and consumption are badly needed. Less polluting and more efficient energy technologies are available, but normally at a higher investment cost than conventional fuels. The international community should play a central role in assisting development country governments in pursuing the goal of digital opportunities for all and to support green technology leapfrogging.

Editor

1

Introduction

The digital convergence of information and communication technologies (ICT) has lessened two long-standing obstacles to communication delay and distance. Ever cheaper, ever more rapid, and ever more varied means of communicating vast amounts of information through the Internet, among other networks, is creating a world in which there is far greater access to information than ever before. Is a "new economy" emerging?

ICT is making access to information more "symmetrical" more people have access to more information whenever and wherever they need it and this is disrupting established economic relations. The effect will be profound changes in the structure of markets and organizations and established patterns of economic behaviour. While much attention has surrounded the volatile new world of the "dot.coms", this is a distraction: the true portent of ICT is how it will transform the "old economy".

Changes in how the economy works will transform the world of work. The creation and loss of jobs, the content and quality of work, the location of work, the nature of the employment contract, the skills required and how often they can be obtained, the organization of work and the functioning and effectiveness of worker and employer organizations all are affected by the emerging era of digital globalization.

Knowledge workers, those who generate ideas and transmit these electronically as "intangible" or "immaterial" products, gain particular advantage in the networking economy: through the Internet and other networking technologies, they have access any time to unlimited amounts of the "raw material" of knowledge creation. Yet there is a knowledge component to all work, and the illiterate farmer can also gain from greater access to information. Nor does networking necessarily mean an increase in knowledge or skill requirements. Unskilled or de-skilled jobs skill polarization in the networking economy also exist.

ICT is a "meta-technology" characterized by pervasive effects on the economy as a whole, and on areas of scientific and technological advance well beyond the ICT sector itself. Barring a disaster scenario, the onrush of information itself is irreversible; however, its course is by no means pre-ordained or pre-determined. This will clearly be a "steerable revolution", in which wise policies and appropriate institutions will be essential toward directing change toward the greatest public good. Passivity will lead to marginalization.

Periods of rapid technological change give rise to innovation and creativity, the outcomes of which cannot be known in advance. One effect of the technologies is clear: work is becoming independent of location and this will change management practices, the nature of the employment contract, and the quality of work. Also, the ability to organize production in "real time" anywhere in the world will no doubt induce changing patterns in the global division of labour.

The digital era has diffused at an astonishing rate. Fifty million people were navigating the Internet within its first four years and their numbers are increasing at a rapid rate. But speed also means disruption and division. Disruption occurs as the inadequacies of existing institutions and regulatory frameworks are exposed to rapid change and new demands. Institutions and organizations that do not adjust risk irrelevance. Technological change always favours the prepared: the world's different speeds of change and different stages of preparedness mean that the existing "digital divides" are certain to widen.

Within countries, the digital divide often has common characteristics. Use of the Internet, for example, is more common among younger than older people, men than women, the more rather than the less educated, urban rather than rural dwellers, and those with higher incomes. One, if not the most significant factor is the level of education, as education itself is related to income and often to location. Girls lag in educational attainment in most countries and, even in wealthy ones, their enrolment in the core courses of the technologies is a small share of boys' enrolment.

Between countries, the divide's features also have common characteristics. Barely 6 per cent of the world's people have ever logged onto the Internet and 85 to 90 per cent of them are in the industrialized countries. The level of national income is strongly related to ICT diffusion and is clearly the distinguishing feature of the divide between industrialized and developing countries.

The cost and availability of telecommunications determines the extent to which the Internet is used, and per capita access costs are most often higher in poorer countries. Coercive governments limit the extent to which information is exchanged, and evidence shows a higher level of Internet usage where political and civil freedoms exist.

Macro-policies and features of the regulatory environment have a determining influence on the degree to which enterprises will adopt new technologies, how they will use them, and whether new enterprises will be created. In general terms, however, it is the incentives that the technologies create at the micro-level and the strong pressure of competition B that will directly determine the economic and employment effects of ICT.

Using ICT lowers costs and can increase productivity economy-wide, including in "old economy" industries. As costs are lowered throughout the economy, some believe that a "new economy" will emerge one characterized by a higher level of potential growth consistent with low inflation. The most that can be said at present is the appearance of a few hopeful signs surrounding the changing price relations associated with ICT. Available evidence does show that electronic markets are more transparent and, through lower transaction costs, appear to result in substantial changes in established price relations. For example, some evidence shows that electronic markets can result in up to 15 per cent lower costs for consumers. It is far more significant that lower costs are also apparent in inter-enterprise or "B2B" transactions across many "old economy" industries. The ICT sector itself is the fastest-growing sector in many industrialized countries. Although the ICT sector usually does not account for much more than 5 per cent of the workforce in any OECD country, the sector's contribution to GDP growth is disproportionately great.

Globalization had already spurred an internal transformation of the enterprise, resulting in changes in the organization of work toward flatter hierarchies and project-based teams. The need for a more rapid response to volatile product markets and declining product life cycles has also been behind the trend toward greater outsourcing. The emerging era of "digital globalization" is accelerating these organizational changes. Enterprises in the most globally competitive industries have experienced both a decline in the time devoted to strategy formulation and a qualitative change in the nature of competitive advantage. "time-to-market" has arisen as a critical competitive asset. This in turn compels companies to rely on the creativity, knowledge, and ability to acquire new knowledge of their core employees.

Evidence shows that major gains in enterprise performance only occur where the use of the new technologies has been combined with wide-ranging changes in work organization. Evidence also shows that the most widespread use of the new technologies exists in enterprises that have adopted the most thorough range of work organization changes, such as the decentralization of decision-making, and the organization of work into semi-autonomous, task-oriented teams.

The fast pace of competition means that, for some highly skilled activities, companies are relying on the external labour market for inputs of temporary duration. The technologies, meanwhile, allow companies to source work independently of location. The outsourcing of needed inputs is accelerated both by the enabling technologies, as well as by competitive pressures. Locations (in both industrialized and developing countries) that have the adequate infrastructure and skills in their labour markets can benefit by participation in new global value chains, in "intangible" product markets such as software development or data processing.

The convergence of "carrier" and "content" industries has resulted in mergers between large firms. At the same time, there are lower barriers to entry in a period of rapidly evolving technologies, in which creativity and innovation matter more than physical plant, physical raw materials, and investment capital. Business start-ups are on the rise.

A world economy integrated in real time carries with it both advantages and new sources of instability. For example, the fortunes of Internet firms and the remuneration of at least some of their workers are unusually dependent on volatile equity markets. Capital markets, meanwhile the most integrated global markets of all through ICT have already proven their ability in recent years to be contributing sources of massive job destruction.

It is also true that value chains integrated in real time create dependencies that, in turn, increase vulnerability to disruption at any stage in the chain. On the one hand, this could prove destabilizing as natural or human-made disturbances anywhere at any one point in a highly integrated chain could have immediate repercussions elsewhere. On the other, another effect of this could well be to increase the leverage that workers and their organizations could bring to bear on the enterprise that employs them.

Finally, a higher level of integration between some developing country locations and industrialized countries could increase the relative exclusion of locations that are not connected. This is another reason why appropriate policies at both international and national levels—involving both the public and private sectors—will be necessary for increasing the gains arising from the use of the technologies.

Productivity growth is greatest in the core ICT sector itself, where, in manufacturing it has resulted in stunning increases in output with nevertheless declining employment. But the employment decline in manufacturing has been more than offset by the rapid growth of new markets and new employment in the service sector, with business and producer services and social services (health, education) claiming the highest share of growth. In France, for example, evidence shows that the negative effects of labour-saving investments in ICT in manufacturing have been largely compensated by job growth in services, business services in particular.

Evidence shows that the countries that have had the greatest growth in "total factor productivity" in the 1990s are those where ICT has been used most widely in the economy. These are also the countries in which employment has grown the most. There is evidence that employment ratios are highest in those countries where the use of ICT is most widespread. Evidence also shows that unemployment has declined most in the small number of countries where Internet use is most widespread, such as Denmark, Finland and Ireland. It is too early to conclude, but there are hopeful signs that the effect of ICT on employment is positive.

Use of the technologies is nevertheless associated with new patterns of job creation and job loss. And despite the hopeful signs of employment creation, it is clear that jobs will also be lost through three main channels obsolescence, automation, and "disintermediation".

ICT replaces old tasks and occupations through automation, such as the telephone switchboard operator. But the technologies also create new tasks and occupations, such as Webpage designers or call-centre workers or a variety of new intermediaries. Consensus reigns on the fact that the highest rates of job creation, job destruction, and job switching occur among the most technologically innovative firms in sectors where overall employment is growing. More generally, ICT creates jobs for occupations in rising demand, such as software programmers, while destroys jobs in those skills in declining demand, such as those associated with analog technologies. Since ICT enables routine tasks to be "codified" and automated as part of the labour-saving increases in productivity that arise with the use of ICT B this, of course, is a source of job loss. Some jobs based on information intermediation travel agents, for example could be lost through more direct access to information or change in function.

Through the Internet and email, when work is independent of location, new ways of working arise. There has been a rise in self-employment. A growing number of "e-lancers" move from enterprise to enterprise or project to project on their own, sometimes for months, sometimes for days. In labour markets that are at the forefront of the digital economy, such as Silicon Valley, the share of self-employed and temporary workers is far higher than the national average. The skill levels and value to the firm of these individuals are high, but the firm specificity of their knowledge is low. In consequence, diversity is increasing in those labour markets where ICT has diffused the most. Although disaggregated data are unavailable, the share of self-employed, temporary and part-time work has been rising in most OECD countries.

The margin of the digital workforce that is mobile has needs that both the reform of existing labour market institutions and the growth of new ones can address. Both public and private employment agencies are extending their range of services beyond the job-matching function to the additional needs of a mobile workforce. While there is substantial variety in the agency work industry, the most advanced companies are not only major providers of career continuity for their temporary workforce, but also providers of skills as well. Trade unions and employer organizations are also offering services to these new independent workers.

The theory that labour markets in the digital era are undergoing profound transformation has some basis in truth. For most people at work, however, there continues to be a surprisingly high degree of employment stability. In 12 out of 16 OECD countries' labour markets, "job tenure", a measure of employment stability, has either remained unchanged during the last decade of the 1990s, or had in fact increased. Even looking more closely at some of the occupations most associated with the "new economy", such as telecommunications workers or those in the distribution sector, job tenure has remained largely unchanged.

Continued employment stability despite an era of fast-paced technological change is not an unreasonable expectation for at least two reasons. First, and as noted earlier, the OECD labour market is ageing. Job tenure always increases with the age of the workforce. A second reason may relate to how ICT and globalization are affecting competitive advantage. As "time-to-market" becomes increasingly important, the organization of work needs to adjust so that a high degree of creativity and a more rapid response to product market pressures can occur. Critical to the new organization of work is the increased need to "tap" the tacit knowledge of the workforce. To do so requires a workplace culture in which trust and experimentation can simultaneously occur. Such behaviours are unlikely to occur between relative strangers in workplaces characterized by a high degree of instability and frequent turnover.

Employment stability is no indication of the absence of change. Labour markets have indeed become more demanding, more diversified, and more turbulent. But most of this turbulence is being internalized with the enterprise, where jobs are indeed changing. Nor does employment stability mean employment security: contracts are changing, stress is on the rise, and there are evidences of employment insecurity perceived by workers up and down the organizational hierarchy.

The places considerable emphasis on the independence of work from any physical location. This is a feature of teleworking from home, but it also refers to the relocation of jobs from industrialized to developing countries, such as "back-office" staff located in call centres, data entry and processing, software development. Work that is independent of location has a growing share of employment in industrialized countries. For example, almost one-fourth of the workforce in the United Kingdom now carries out at least some of its work at home. By 2003, there will be an estimated 1.3 million employed in call centres in the European Union, up from an estimated 670,000 in 2001. Women are often thought to benefit from the new independence of work location.

In some ways, this is clearly the case: working from home, for example, can allow a better accommodation of work and family schedules. But isolation and exclusion from career choices can also occur. Women tend less than men to mix telework with stays at the office. Nor is women's telework as mobile as men's, but concentrated at home. At home, women are more likely to combine telework with family responsibilities, whereas men are more likely to separate the two. Call centres and data processing in developing countries are predominantly female occupations. But data processing, although it may be better than other local labour market alternatives, may not lead to career upgrading. And wages and conditions of work in call centres appear to vary widely. In the best, a new, more informal and more appealing work culture may be apparent; but, in the worst instances, call centres have been called the "sweatshops of the digital era".

One estimate suggests that up to 5 per cent of all service-sector jobs in industrialized countries could be "contestable" by developing countries. This would amount to about 12 million jobs in which relocation to developing countries could occur. For example, in the Caribbean countries, almost 5,000 women were employed in data processing activities in the late 1990s. Such jobs can provide developing countries with an important toehold in global export markets, as well as providing direct employment and foreign exchange earnings. But if the magnitude of the relocation of work is a credible estimate, it implies that the greatest employment potential of ICT for developing countries needs to lie elsewhere. Beyond participation in global value chains through the increasing tradability of services, the technologies offer the chance for purely domestic activities and associated job growth.

Through telecentres, for example, countries such as Bangladesh, India and Senegal and others have been able to create direct employment for thousands of women and men. Over the last four years in India, for example, an estimated 250,000 jobs for women have been created through mobile telephony centres. Such local entrepreneurial activities are likely to have positive externalities on local economies as well. Evidence also shows that women's operation of telecentres increases the participation of women as consumers of these services.

It is clear that ICT is merely a tool, and tools do not substitute for genuine development. ICT, however, offer tools that may accelerate development. Since the principal consequence of ICT is greater access to and use of information, it is precisely those locations that have the least of both where the technologies could have the greatest marginal impact. Telecommunications are positively correlated with economic growth. Even mobile telephony can be a stimulus to local economic development and, in causal terms, some evidence shows that better telecommunications are likely to be a source of economic growth. A widening digital divide may be inevitable, but using the technologies can be beneficial at any level of economic development. The potential welfare gains for developing countries are of three major types are given below:

— Countries with the right mix of skills, infrastructure, and policies could become important locations in global markets for intangible products or ICT products generally. Countries as diverse as Brazil, China, Costa Rica, Israel, Malaysia and Romania have all been able to gain niches in such markets. Some commonalities underlie their success. It is clear, for example, that for maximum gains to emerge, the development of essential ICT skills, including software development, is necessary. Without such skills, the technologies can neither be maintained nor adapted to local usages, from which greater economic advantages are obtained.

— Acceleration of development can occur through the leapfrogging potentials inherent in the technologies, where leapfrogging is defined as the ability to bypass earlier investments in the time or cost of development. Leapfrogging has first of all a technological foundation: through wireless applications, developing countries can bypass more costly and time-consuming investments in fixed-wire telecom infrastructures. In economic terms, leapfrogging can occur through several channels. For example, developing countries have often gained an initial niche in export markets through comparative advantage in cheap, unskilled labour, as is characteristic of the garment industry. Where appropriate skills are available, countries can now bypass this earlier, lower value-added entrance into global markets in favour of greater value-added production. An example is Costa Rica, where the educational level of the workforce was a vital factor in Intel's decision to locate a semiconductor production facility. Small enterprises in developing countries have at least potential access to a global market for both tangible and intangible products. For example, pockets of software development are now occurring in the Philippines and in Viet Nam for clients identified through the Internet. For tangible products, provided that the physical infrastructure is adequate enough for the fulfilment of transactions to occur, countries can find markets for goods in which they have an unassailable competitive advantage, such as products made locally or cultural artefacts. In many cases, leapfrogging refers to advantages at the microeconomic level. For macroeconomic gains to occur requires a range of commercial, trade, investment, telecommunications and other infrastructure policies to be brought to bear on the development potential of ICT. China's strategy is particularly promising in this regard. It has combined previously separate ministries into the Ministry of Information Industries, and established economic zones particularly devoted to the growth of start-up ICT ventures.

— The third welfare gain that could underpin a new development paradigm arises from the possibilities that networking opens up for poverty alleviation. To the extent that ICT can improve aggregate economic growth, this could generate linkages to activities that provide livelihoods for those who are poor. Poor people could also benefit directly through access to the information that the technologies provide or through the potential for greater collective voice and empowerment they allow.

— To the extent that the technologies can make governments more transparent, extend their services more broadly, and at lower cost, the poor could benefit from the improved quality and reach of health, education and social services. This could also create opportunities for women through access to learning, incomes, and greater autonomy. Access to ICT for poor segments of the population is likeliest to occur at the community level. A key focus for expanding such access could be through the improvement of NGO capacities and other local development agencies in, for example, the fields of health care, child welfare, or basic education or nutrition.

ICT and Education

Literacy and education cannot be leapfrogged, yet both are vital for reaping the greatest advantages from the emerging digital era. The promotion of education and literacy generally, and digital literacy in particular, is a challenge facing all countries. Educational differences underlie the different rates of penetration of ICT and Internet usage. For example, the ICT world is often depicted as a world of relatively young men, and the available evidence supports this depiction. Two-thirds of the world's illiterate are girls and women. Nor are girls sufficiently enrolled in the science curricula at the core of the technologies' innovation and use.

In the wealthiest countries, substantial progress has been made in ensuring access to the Internet in school rooms. The European Union's programme, for example, is for 100 per cent "connectivity" in schools by the end of 2001. Access alone is insufficient: teachers need to be trained in the substance of the new technologies and their most effective use. Even in the wealthiest countries, such training is far from thorough, and investments in the pursuit of this objective are often minimal. Obviously, for the majority of the world's people, this objective is distant from reality. In the poorest countries, the main objectives need to continue to be the promotion of literacy and access to general education.

Poorly equipped schools or their absence altogether are most characteristic of the poorest locations. Through their application to distance-learning, the technologies could greatly multiply access to learning opportunities for those who most need them. Distance learning applications, while costly to develop, have low unit costs the more there are people who use them. In such locations, distance learning can be an important complement to existing education providers.

Wealth creation in the wealthiest countries relies less on physical inputs than on knowledge. The frontiers of knowledge itself, however, are rapidly expanding. Two consequences of this are, first, a shift in teaching methodologies away from the transfer of facts to students as passive recipients, and, instead, towards teaching students how to learn and instilling in them the curiosity to do so. In short, how people learn is becoming as important as what they learn. A parallel trend is observable in high tech firms exposed to fast-paced competition. The ability to learn, to transform existing knowledge into new knowledge, is a source of competitive advantage of increasing significance. In such companies, daily learning has become an integral part of the job. Part of such learning relies on the exchange of tacit knowledge among employees.

The adoption of ICT in enterprises is creating two types of skill needs. The first relates to a variety of foundation skills, such as the ability to learn, to communicate, and to analyse and solve problems, all of which are essential to work environments that rely on rapid innovation, and the interpersonal exchange and creation of knowledge. Beyond such skills, however, are the technical skills related to ICT itself, the need for which extends well beyond the ICT sector to the economy as a whole.

Where the technologies are most broadly in use, skill shortages particularly in the technical support skills surrounding both hardware and software applications are acute, if difficult to quantify. This, in turn, is a brake on economic growth for enterprises that would otherwise adopt the technologies' applications more readily. Three problems relating to the skills shortage are of particular significance. The first of these is the debate over labour migration. The availability of technical skills in developing countries could be used to meet the skill needs of industrialized countries.

On the positive side, migrant workers benefit from the greater experience and higher wages that migration can bring, and sending countries can benefit from the remittances their expatriates send home. It is also true that countries such as China, India and Viet Nam have all benefited from the networks their expatriates have created outside the country, and also from the skills and experiences they repatriate when they do return home. For receiving countries, of course, reliance on foreign labour is a way of overcoming skill shortages in the short term.On the negative side, however, the outward migration of the technically skilled can result in a brain drain, depriving developing countries of these scarce skills. For example, possibly all of India's annual graduates in ICT-related core skills could be in demand in industrialized countries. For receiving countries, meanwhile, there are two problems.

— Some evidence suggests that the attractiveness of skilled migrant labour in the United States comes from the lower pay that employers can offer them relative to domestic labour. Additionally, there is concern in both the United States as well as in European Union countries that recourse to foreign labour might detract from the need for the training and retraining of the existing workforce. This is particularly the case where emerging skill shortages coexist with still relatively high unemployment.

— The ageing workforce in many OECD countries. This implies, first of all, that the majority of "tomorrow's workforce" is, in fact, already on the job. The promotion of lifelong learning and the retraining of the existing workforce need therefore to be policy objectives applied to those already at work. Equipping workers with ICT-related skills, therefore, will need to be specifically targeted to the needs of older workers.

— The possibility of a skills polarization emerging as the technologies are taken up by enterprises. On the high end, highly skilled workers using ICT-related skills intensively on the job may have broad career options and command high salaries. But there remain many jobs in the networking economy that are low-skilled and low-paid. The polarization of skills could also reinforce the gender-based segmentation of the labour market.

There are many avenues available to address the greater need for retraining and lifelong learning. Both feature prominently in enterprise training policies, as well as in the strategies of trade unions, and access to learning opportunities increasingly features in national tripartite agreements or at the collective bargaining table. In Singapore, for example, the Critical Enabling Skills Training (CREST) programme will enrol 100,000 trainees in 2001. Germany's tripartite Alliance for Jobs agreed on the creation of training places for 60,000 people in ICT up to 2003. In South Africa, a tripartite training authority in the ICT sector specifically was set up in 2000.

Addressing the skills shortage has resulted in new ways in which training is delivered and new deliverers of that training. Distance-learning is a valuable substitute for classroom instruction. For example, multinational enterprises are increasingly using distance learning applications for their staff worldwide: in an environment of rapid change, lifelong learning has become critical to corporate success, as well as to the employability of workers. Classrooms are a poor substitute for learning vehicles that can be used anywhere, anytime, such as distance-learning. Evidence also suggests that interactive, multimedia formats can often be a more effective means of knowledge retention than classroom lectures. To remedy a worldwide shortage of skills in ICT makes good economic sense and will require both an innovative new range of public/private partnerships as well as investments of human and financial resources.

Will the quality of work and life improve? The networking economy offers genuine potential for striking a better balance between work and family responsibilities, or work and leisure. Work itself has become more rewarding for many in its pay and in its content. The creation and use of knowledge on the job can be inherently more satisfying than the monotony of narrow tasks performed under strict supervision. The independence of work from its location can be liberating not only in spatial terms, but also in the ability to schedule work when desired. The increasing knowledge content of work should favour the equality of women and men in the workforce. Intelligence and creativity are also homogeneously distributed between industrialized and developing countries, or between people with and without physical disabilities. The digital era's potential to improve the quality of work and life is clearly real. But it is not a given. The values, agreements, and institutions of an earlier industrial era are often no longer suited to current trends in working conditions. Gaps in social protection are opening up.

Some of the self-employed, for example, are in disguised self-employment, dependent on an individual employer but without the benefits of an employment contract. Also, as stimulating as work can be in fast-paced, semi-autonomous work teams, not all workers are likely to appreciate the greater risks associated with greater responsibility. These risks extend from the need to keep oneself employable through continuous learning to the greater stress of having simultaneously to manage competing demands, cope with information overload, etc.

An irony of the communications revolution, moreover, is that a sharply higher intensity of virtual communications can go hand in hand with increased isolation. That much work in the digital era can be done anywhere, anytime has meant for some that this is precisely what is occurring, with a consequent blurring of hours or work and hours of leisure. Far from adjusting working needs to the needs of family life, there can be rising pressure to work everywhere and all the time. Older workers could be excluded from the new careers and opportunities created by the technologies, and women, too, as they lag behind men in scientific and technical training.

Addressing the negative consequences of changes in the nature of work has been the key function of industrial relations. In creating a more diversified labour market, however, the diffusion of these technologies renders the effort of collective organization and representation far more difficult. The technologies are associated with smaller units of production and they accelerate both the trend toward outsourcing, as well as the frequent redefinition of who is a core employee and who is not.

Fragmentation in the organization of production, and a continually changing organization of work, are additional challenges to organizing workers in the new economy. The effects of ICT on the quality of life at work have strong potentials in both positive and negative directions. It is clear that the need for worker protection remains and is arguably greater in the context of the disruptive changes that are occurring.

There is evidence of the need for changing attitudes and strategies within the trade union movement to address issues of organizing and the representation of new areas of worker protection. Some international trade secretariats, such as the Union Network International (UNI), have comprehensive strategies and programmes in place for the networking economy. For example, UNI's "online rights for online workers" campaign emphasizes employee representatives' right to corporate email and intranet communications, and the right for privacy and due process in the monitoring of employee communications.

Various of the risks to the quality of life at work are also being addressed by trade unions in their policies, bargaining agreements, or tripartite negotiations. Of these, the right to lifelong learning and access to such opportunities is perhaps the most fundamental, and one where substantial progress is being made. In recognition of the fact that teleworking creates welcome opportunities for some employees but also risks it, too, is an area in which collective bargaining is extensive.

Common features in telework agreements include that it be undertaken voluntarily, that the worker's decision is reversible, and that the pay and employment status of the teleworker are not downgraded. The issue of stress at the workplace is also beginning to enter the bargaining agendas of trade unions. The digital reproduction of intellectual property is a concern of workers in the entertainment and media interests, and a focus of bargaining for journalists.

Trade unions are also addressing the digital divide through expanding access to the new technologies. Both the Swedish LO and the AFL-CIO in the United States, for example, assist in the effort to overcome the within-country digital divide through the provision of low-cost, Internet-connected PCs to members. International trade secretariats are also assisting their affiliates in developing countries to become digitally literate.

However much it may be the case that the present era of technological change presents certain risks to labour market institutions, the technologies can also be of benefit to trade unions and employer organizations. For example, some employer organizations, such as ALMEGA in Sweden, have created an online presence a "virtual employers' organization" allowing them to provide interactive services, individually tailored to members' interests.

The Web allows them to reach out to non-members as well, particularly the new small firms in the new economy. For trade unions, the fundamental aim remains that of organizing the new, more diverse ICT workforce. UNI has targeted the organizing of freelance workers as a priority area, for example. Some trade unions have established organizations especially for the self-employed. In the Netherlands, the Allied Union in the FNV federation created the FNV Zelfstandige Bondgenoten in 1999, the first Dutch trade union specifically for self-employed people.

In the United States, a variant of the "guild model" of organization is being experimented with by a newly formed organization affiliated to the Communication Workers of America: the Washington Alliance of Technology Workers (WashTech) is a new Web-based service provider for agency and directly employed workers in the ICT sector, offering individual services, rather than collective bargaining. Access to information and the collective strength of communication can assist trade unions in redressing imbalances of power in the workplace.

The Internet was the vehicle through which the Seattle protests against the World Trade Organization meeting in 1999 were organized. There are also numerous examples of how the Internet has been used to increase the "symmetry of information" at the bargaining table. Through the Internet, local disputes can "go global". Many trade unions have engaged in "cyber-pickets" to shed light broadly on violations of worker rights and bad industrial relations practices. In a global organization of production that increasingly relies on information flows in real time, giving greater leverage to the voice of workers is a clear possibility.

The issue of policies needed to increase the potential gains of the emerging digital era and lessen the costs of adjustment. The positive potential of the technologies for employment growth, a better quality of life, and as a tool for reinforcing the development agenda is beyond doubt. Not beyond doubt is whether this potential can be translated into reality for the majority of the world's people anytime soon - or whether the risks of change can be avoided. A passive policy stance that leaves to markets alone the direction of change will reinforce divides. It is also the case that the quality of life and work for women and men will be exposed as much to the potential for negative outcomes as positive ones. For all these reasons, social choices and the social institutions through which such choices are moulded are essential to the digital era.

2

Opportunities of Digital Technologies

Information and Communication Technology (ICT) is, in many ways, a unique technology. It has the characteristic of a threshold technology, with the ability to rapidly change the whole structure of society and reshape the way our economy is organised. It is probably not an overstatement to say that the change our economy and technological systems has entered into is of the magnitude of the industrial revolution of the eighteenth century, or even of that of the prehistoric agricultural revolution.

As an interactive technology that fundamentally changes ways and means of communication ICT will also create a cultural revolution, a revolution that could have a significant impact upon the way we perceive ourselves and the world, similar to the impact caused by the Copernican and Darwinian revolutions. However positive the uses of this technology can be if aimed in a sustainable direction, it is important to acknowledge that ICT is not a panacea to the world's environmental and social problems. No matter how we use this technology, our society will continue to have an environmental impact upon the world and social tensions will continue to exist.

There is no such thing as a weightless or friction-less economy: mankind will always need food and shelter, will own material objects, and will need transport for these as well as for itself. All these activities will have an environmental impact. In the same way, ICT will result in new social situations where new actors emerge and new values are shaped. Even if the new society will be more just and equitable, people's views on how society should develop will still differ, as will their influence. Although this might seem obvious, discussions about ICT too often seem to forget that the "new "society is squarely based on the foundation of the traditional society.

When society is transformed from an industrial to an information-based economy, the problems of the industrial society will not vanish, since most parts of this society will still exist, even if in a different form. The information society will be layered atop the industrial society in the same way that the industrial society is layered over the agricultural society. Needless to say, the development of the new form of economy will not take place simultaneously all over the planet, nor look the same everywhere. It is therefore pointless to try and draw a distinct line between the so-called old and new economy, as this blurred line is drawn in time, includes all sectors and contains gradual changes mixed with sudden shifts.

As the infrastructure for this new society begins to come into place, there is, a unique opportunity to shape the whole system in a way coherent to humanity's needs and visions for the future. Thus, while it is important to find the economic, social and environmental triple-win situation today, it is even more important to find in which way to direct development in order to create a structure where most situations have such successful possible outcomes. The complexity of ICT makes it difficult to approach in a traditional manner, which focuses only on the direct impacts of extraction, manufacturing, use, and disposal. It is vital that all due caution be taken when responding to ICT-based challenges.

The impact of ICT must be viewed in a very broad sense, from cultural changes caused by the use of new technologies, to the appearance of new possibilities for shaping a new economy in which production and consumption patterns look fundamentally different.

The impact of E-shopping, for example, cannot be reduced to the computers used for the transactions, or even to the eliminated car trip to the store. Instead, the whole distribution chain must be examined to determine what kind of long term impact this kind of consumption will have on the economy, the development of the infrastructure, as well as upon habits.

To complicate things further, the development of ICT will also create new economic, legal and cultural "meta challenges ". Not only must society learn to think in new ways when working with ICTs, but existing factors, institutions and sectors will have to rearrange themselves.

Some of these participants must abandon areas that they used to dominate, and others must expand their field of responsibility -and obviously new institutions and networks will need to be created during this process.

As the speed of change is so fast, the need for flexible measures and the ability to allow new ideas the room to evolve will be very important. At the same time, a period of rapid change tends to frighten both people and institutions into defensive positions, in which it seems easiest to revert to well-known ways of thinking and well-known ways of work. This creates a challenging situation where the need for new thinking and for new ways of solving problems will be confronted with groups trying to protect what they control today, fearful of losing influence in a society with new ground rules and new goals.

It is impossible, and therefore unwise, to try to give a final answer to the question of how to direct ICT development so that it supports sustainable development. Notwithstanding that total solutions have always led societies into dead ends, the rapid change society is going through will make all specific recommendations outdated before they can be applied. A beginning can, however, be made by developing a framework for sustainable ICT development; and in doing that we can hopefully create an atmosphere in which a critical mass of different actors start to move in a sustainable direction.

In an attempt to inspire a discussion about the prerequisite for a sustainable framework where ICT is a part of the solution instead of the problem, this text will go through three steps. First, we will look at two overarching questions that must be discussed by all actors in society. After that, four sustainable ICT principles will be introduced as a guide for drafting long term strategies in different areas, including the private and public sector, as well as civil society. Finally, seven strategic areas for ICT are presented, focusing attention on a number of strategic challenges. Progress in these areas, or lack of it, will be an indicator of whether the use of ICT is contributing to a society that moves in a sustainable direction or not.

Before discussing ICT and democracy, it is helpful to step back and look at the original meaning of democracy. The word derives from the Greek word demokratia, a combination of demos, "people ",and kratos, "rule ". Hence, democracy strictly means rule by the many instead of by the few, based on the belief that everyone in society should have the same basic rights and freedoms and that people should be free to govern themselves. Today most democratic nations are representative democracies, where the people elect public officials, with the expectation that the latter act according to the desires of the people. Popular sovereignty is still supposed to be at the heart of democracy, with the wishes of the people supreme, and not the individual leaders, political parties or groups with money and power.

Many of the trends seen today contrast the manner in which democracy is ensured with new challenges. For example, many large corporations grow fast and already have significantly more resources than many developing countries, the technological development is fast and complex, new ways of communication are dominated by certain participants within society, and there are multiple threats to the planet that cannot be solved on a local or national level. Democracy and the democratic framework needs to evolve to be able to face such supranational issues.

With the growth of ICT, all societies, whether democratic or not, have been given a new context. The opportunities and challenges for democracy are significant, and of different kinds, which may be divided for convenience into three different groups: the first relative to the technological and economical situation, the second to information and knowledge, and the third to the cultural environment.

An important technological and economic challenge, and one that is frequently mentioned in the context of democracy, is access to the technological tools that help find information and communicate. If ICT is to be used as a democratic medium, every citizen must have easy and affordable access to ICT-enabled products. At the global level, the need for action is obvious. International negotiations affecting everyone on this planet are frequently developed in different drafts that are circulated, discussed and commented on over the Internet. This has created a situation where anyone who wants to take part in the development of the global framework, including the development of ICT, must have access to ICT. At the same time, it is obvious that many of those who really need to be a part of these discussions do not have access to ICT.

One of the groups excluded from these discussions are the world's poorest countries. Their biggest problem, however, is usually not access to ICT, but the lack of capacity to process all the information to which it gives access. This is partly due to their lack of ICT infrastructure and equipment, but also to the lack of other basic resources. When looking at exclusion from an individual perspective, it becomes clear that we must go beyond the country and state perspective when addressing excluded groups. Small and medium size enterprises, small scale farmers, the unemployed, young people, ethnic minorities, and those with values difficult or impossible to assess in monetary terms, are all groups that have difficulty participating in the discussions that shape the global framework due to their exclusion. Many of these groups come from economically disadvantaged countries, but far from all.

In a global society, with many challenges facing humanity, it is difficult to envisage a situation where democracy is the guiding principle without ensuring that each and everyone can make their voice heard. With ICT becoming a necessary tool for influencing and participating in the development of the policies and organisations that will shape the future, as well as a tool for sharing information between citizens, universal highspeed access must be placed high up on the international agenda.

Naturally, traditional basic needs must also be addressed. However, instead of treating access and the ability to communicate as a luxury, as is frequently the case today, it must be considered as a fundamental pillar of any serious development policy.

A second, less frequently discussed but no less important challenge for democracy is linked to the rapid technological development of ICT. ICT is an integrated part of a broader technological development, including tailor-made chemicals, biotechnology, robotics, quantum computing and nanotechnology.

New groundbreaking innovations can be expected to come out of research laboratories in the near future, with others already available on a large scale. A key challenge is how to democratically aim the development of these technologies in a direction that support sustainable development. With an economy that demands fast and high rates of return, incentives increase to put new technologies on the market before properly discussing and assessing their social and environmental impact. The use of ICT could, if used in the right way, facilitate and speed up proper assessment of new technologies, as well as a broader discussion of the current technological development.

Today there are good arguments for the current system from a traditional economic perspective, such as economy of scale, but for democratic reasons incentives should be considered that even out the market for other, less complex and locally developed solutions. This is not to say that centralised high-tech solutions could not have an important part to play, but that other approaches also should be encouraged in order to find sustainable solutions.

The broad introduction of ICT has already fundamentally changed the ways information is used, processed and disseminated. Historically, political and economic systems used to work within a timeframe of a few years and sometimes months.

During the Industrial Age, elections and annual reports were the events around which the important decisions of modern democracies have revolved. This limited timeframe has, however, often proven inadequate to deal with many of the challenges that affect nature and future generations, especially when looking years, decades, or even centuries ahead. As ICT spreads through all levels of society, the pace of economic and political decisions has accelerated even further.

Today reactions on the stock market and opinion polls pressurise many groups into using time frames of weeks, days or even hours. The introduction of information technology over the last few years has for example made it possible for global financial markets and others to react and act within minutes, or even seconds, to different events around the planet. Thus, when something happens that affects the economy, the large financial and economic actors usually react in a matter of minutes, followed by the media, then by a political decision in response to the media and pressure from different groups, followed by another market reaction, then by another media reaction.

The need for rapid response increases as the social changes accelerate and different groups try to process new information. In this situation, it is easy to portray the potential responses to the challenges in a dichotomised manner, since there is little time for reflection. This trend is frequently encouraged by the mass media, where a simple and overly dramatic approach built on familiar and well-known ideas is often considered the best. In a democratic society that must take decision regarding complex questions with far reaching consequences this is, however, a dangerous tendency, as it discourages dialogue and the understanding of different and new perspectives.

Sometimes the actual social and environmental implications do not even influence the process where the different actors try to foresee the next move of the other actors without checking out what the real implications are. As the real world is influenced by the reactions on the market, political decisions and how media portray reality, today's society is in a situation where the relation between fiction and reality often are difficult to understand. Some would even claim that it is impossible to uphold the traditional idea of a difference between the real and the virtual. ICT solutions need to be democratically encouraged so as to create a situation where actors with different perspectives can meet, and where the general public can get information about what these different groups decide upon, whilst reflecting both sides of the debate.

Historically, democratic societies have been organised around certain geographical boundaries, where nations, states and corporations exist. However, modern democracy is a relatively recent invention, and has not been around for more than 200 years, even if the concept that a free people should govern itself has been in existence for more than 2000 years. The current structure of society, including representative democracy, is something that to a great extent was created as a response to the industrialisation process that took place during the last two centuries, and was thus imposed from above on nations and states that had evolved from feudalistic concepts.

Globalisation has brought many changes to current institutions. Many new challenges requiring a solution are global or regional. A large number of transnational corporations have become increasingly powerful, and may act with little concern for national borders. An increasing number of individuals are also part of different international networks, through their profession or personal interest.

In many cases, traditional borders today can be said to be of little or no interest - and where there is no national context, a culture is created in which people's identity and interests do not necessarily coincide with national or local geographical boundaries. In this situation, it is not surprising that the role of the existing structures, including democratically elected governments, are now being questioned.

Many groups trying to achieve specific objectives, in environmental, social and other matters, have also shifted their attention from democratically elected institutions and have turned towards large corporations. By its fundamentally networked nature, ICT brings people together and enables groups to meet their objectives without necessarily going through the traditional democratic structures. This could potentially enhance democracy in the future, but could also undermine the current structures that are intended to guarantee democratic development, without replacing it with a new democratic structure.

Many special interest groups have clear and specific objectives, such as human rights, certain environmental problems, or in the case with corporations, profit. Of these groups, very few are engaged in broader issues that deal with the future of our democracy.

The result is that many of these factors, in most cases unintentionally, erode the old democratic structures without replacing them with new democratic structures. Another challenge relates to the kind of information that ICT helps to spread. So far, those economies wherein most hardware and software used for ICT are developed have focused on satisfying mainly material needs.

These material needs are satisfied thanks to two types of information: first, "coping information ",the kind of information needed for basic survival; second, "helping information ",i.e. how to survive in the most efficient way. This last kind of information has ripened to an extreme extent in the current economic system, coming to include almost all economic information that perceives individuals as customers for any nebulous product.

"Empowering information "is required in order to build relationships between people, and to facilitate the development of human beings in everyday life. There is also a need for "edifying information " or "wisdom ".This last category includes more reflective and transcending experiences, ethical or philosophical information that has to do with moral and ethical questions.

A society needs all these different kinds of information, and different structures for distributing them. Unfortunately, the different kinds of information are often considered as dichotomous, when they should be looked upon as complementary.

Food, shelter and other basic necessities are a pre-requirement to having time to consider questions about relationships and the meaning of life. However, in materialistic societies, moral and ethical questions often end up neglected. It is interesting to observe that specific cultures with much less material welfare than western society seem to have developed further in regard to perceptions of non-material and consumerist issues. If a sustainable democratic society is to evolve, which includes time for reflection upon ethical questions, an economic system is required that can deliver enough material goods for all as well as give room to broader human development.

There is no "right " answer when it comes making choices for tomorrow's society, and there is a significant need for democratic arenas in which to discuss the choices faced. Fora and platforms should be created where different stakeholders can meet and discuss the opportunities and challenges that ICT brings on all different levels; local, national, regional, and global.

In the process of developing the new democratic framework, we must not limit ourselves to the traditional structures: instead, different networks should be created, focusing on different areas, creating global clearinghouses for ideas and needs. At the same time, existing democratic institutions should be consistently respected, whilst developing the current system into a structure that can cope with new challenges.

Mankind's primary focus in many regions is no longer simply upon survival. Unfortunately, the way in which this situation was achieved is far from perfect, and the rest of the world cannot develop along the same path if an ecological and social disaster is to be avoided. The fact is that if every human alive today consumed natural resources and emitted carbon dioxide at the same rate as the average American, German or Frenchman, at least another two earths would be required for this to be sustained for any length of time.

As new technologies evolve, the possibility for a highly integrated global economy has emerged. However, economic development in different parts of the globe will naturally not be a carbon copy of western societies industrialisation process. The question then is what will global, regional and local development look like in an economy where the material needs of the world's population are met within the carrying capacity of the planet. It is in this dynamic and complex situation that ICT can play a crucial role.

Approaching the question of ICTs role for a sustainable economy, two points must be kept in mind. First, there should be a balance between marginal changes and structural changes when trying to direct current economy in a sustainable direction. Secondly, ICT must be used in a flexible way, depending on the specific situation, in order to meet very different needs in different parts of the word, while still working in an economy where the interdependence is high.

ICT has the capacity to dematerialise certain products, such as CDs and books, and turn them into services delivered by electrons instead of atoms. ICT can also make many current processes more efficient by supporting more and better information. The way information is processed and shared opens up new possibilities to pooling problem-solving capacities. New ways to monitor different processes could also open up new ways of responding more accurately and faster to problems as they emerge. These would be important steps forward, but are still insufficient to achieve long term sustainable development for all people on this planet.

Marginal improvements in the existing system must therefore be complemented by structural changes. This is even more crucial as some marginal improvements in evidence today are counterproductive. Instead of being a step towards sustainability, these counterproductive marginal improvements lead to dead ends where resources are wasted in bolstering a system that cannot be further improved.Many of ICTs most important contribution to sustainability will therefore take place when it contributes to a structural shift of our current economy, requiring a new use of ICT in our infrastructure systems like transport, housing, agriculture and energy production. In order to reap the full potential of ICT there must also be a progress away from the industrial perspective where human beings are reduced to being either a part in a production chain or a consumer.

In a post-industrial society, human beings should be seen as creative citizens with dreams and visions, and the economy as nothing more than a tool to realise these dreams and visions. When it is said that politics are dead or that we have reached the end of history, it might be of some relevance in the context of the old structures of the modern industrial society, but when looking at ICT and the future beyond the industrial society, nothing could be more wrong.

The chance for change must be seen in today's context, where ICT is being developed in societies that still seem unwilling to move away from a single minded focus on "more ". GDP growth is still widely used as a measure of development and progress, although there is a clear need to further qualify what "more "is required. Even if there are attempts to improve the current growth paradigm, most institutions still encourage increased consumption and more production relentlessly, and do so without any tools separating desirable growth from unwanted and negative developments.

It is clear that in western countries, the emphasis must be shifted away from providing more material goods to providing better and smarter services. In this process. The economic system must be modified, with new indicators providing a more correct picture of the state of society than do today's "compasses ",such as Gross Domestic Product (GDP). With networked technology providing more and better information about the state of the economy, there is also less need for simplified and aggregated economic measurements that do not necessarily show the whole picture.

The future of ICT could be a part of what would be one of the most important steps in mankind's history; a step away from a society focused on material needs, towards a society engaged in pursuing that which gives life a moral and ethical meaning. In this process. The economy must be viewed as a mere tool for the creation of welfare, material goods and services that simplify personal development.

In relation to the world's poorer countries, ICT faces important challenges. It must contribute to bringing together all parts of the world to reach a situation in which every individual can meet their basic needs. As the more economically disadvantaged parts of the world cannot take the same developmental path as those that are already industrially developed, ways must be found for these countries and regions to leapfrog economically and socially over the more wasteful and polluting societies. If this does not take place, the current loss of valuable nature and the extinction of species will not only accelerate, but increased tensions within and between countries, the haves and the have-nots, will be created, causing potential flash-points for conflict, and worse.

The biggest danger on the global level from a sustainability perspective is if ICT only will be used to make the existing economy more efficient. As influential groups might try to use ICT in order to reap short term benefits, globally targeted policies must be carefully developed so as not to create the wrong incentives, since this could worsen the current negative social, economic an ecological trends.

The complexity of the different societies in the world existing in parallel with different needs must not prevent action. As the world becomes more economically integrated, the need for specific and targeted solutions will most likely increase. In this situation, simple solutions such as "free trade "or "economic growth "must be used with caution. If history has one lesson to teach, it is to be careful with simple and "obvious "solutions.

As for global institutions, the challenge is significant, as they have to address different kind of needs. There are still large areas of the world that lack fundamental services, food, housing, medical care, etc, and those may still use parts of the old economic models in their development process, whilst incorporating environmental and social aspects. At the same time, other areas need to redirect their economy away from material production and consumption.

Many actors, new inventions, new values and unforeseen events are interacting with each other and, often with the help of ICT networks on different levels, cross-pollinating each other. What makes current developments even harder to direct is that there is not merely rapid development along several different paths, but also a situation in which the entire system, as well as parts of the system, are in the process of leaping from one level of importance to another. Different subjects, organisations and technologies that have existed on the margins are therefore all of a sudden becoming the centre of attention.

In a society where the economy has been designed to solve the problems of material scarcity, the focus revolves around maximising the material output. Most existing structures and institutions in the industrial society are therefore formed to maximise the production and distribution of basic material needs, such as food, housing and medicine.

Today, when large parts of society have their material needs satisfied, the situation is different, and the provision of services has come to the fore. Two issues must, however, be highlighted:

First, the existing focus on "more "has resulted in a wasteful economy that barely acknowledges Nature or social concerns. This system is not sustainable, and needs to be entirely rethought in order to lift the whole world to a sufficient level of material welfare, whilst remaining ecologically and socially sustainable, and providing the more intangible benefits of a society where more ethical concerns are the focus.

Second, and even more importantly, in the more affluent parts of the world, most people do not need more products in order to increase their welfare. They might need better products, but far more often what is required is better services, or that which has become the most precious commodity in our society: time. In order to change today's society and culture to one focusing on quality and service, a paradigm shift is required. This shift, would, however, be more linked to changing mores than to the external and superficial aspect of institutions.

Every product that exists or is planned should be examined to determine whether the service provided by the product is a necessary one, and the best manner in which to deliver that service. If this is the angle taken from the beginning, a more dynamic environment will be created where people, institutions and corporations do not feel tied to a certain way of delivering a service.

Investigating the substitution by services of today's products, a number of important improvements can clearly be achieved, however, they will remain marginal. In addressing most of today's important issues, the larger infra-structural systems also need to be examined. Two situations in which a change in focus could have dramatic repercussions for the environment are: the production of energy, and the provision of transport.

Almost all participants involved in today's energy systems focus on energy production, and not on sustainable energy services. With regard to the transport system, the responsible departments in governments and the corporations involved all have their focus on physical transport, and most specifically on transport by road.

By shifting focus, the emphasis could be changed: instead of coal, oil, fossil gas and nuclear power, energy services themselves would be the hub; instead of cars or even transportation, communication would be the focus. This change of focus can be relatively simple, as demonstrated by an increasing number of participants within these industries who see the possibilities in this change, but it is hard to change structures wherein "experts "have invested much of their time, energy, and pride.

With regard to the transport industry, an airline might transform itself into a meeting company and introduce videoconferences as a complement to the traditional business, while another might define itself as a transport company and look for sustainable ways to transport goods and people. In the same way, one manufacturer of fridges might shift to become a supplier of cool space, and another supply fresh nutritious ecological food.

As technological breakthroughs make new things possible, the need should be communicated and prioritised for solutions that could make the different systems truly sustainable. There is often a reluctance today to admit that current systems are far from sustainable, with the result that it is hard for other participants in society to see what kind of needs exist and how to contribute to sustainable development.

Today's economic system creates frustration, and much indicates that many would like to live in a culture where more room is left for reflection, participation and discussion. ICTs role in enhancing these elements will be a great opportunity for change, despite many traditional influential actors seeing this as a threat to their short term profit. On the other hand, many would probably enjoy the challenge of solving many of today's problems, and of being a part of a cultural change where "quantity "is left behind, and a new focus put on "quality ". If we are to shift from a product-focused society to a service-orientated one, we must look at what kind of culture is promoted by the ICT system.

As the ICT-system develops, there must be room for values beside consumerism. If those using ICT are treated only as consumers and never as citizens, a global ICT-network might turn out to be the biggest threat to sustainability ever encountered. A global culture based upon the frustrating feeling of not being able to consume as much as wanted, and with little or no time for reflection and discussion about other values or the future of society, leads a clear comparison with Aldous Huxley's "Brave New World ". When a new technology is introduced in a rapidly changing environment, unexpected problems should be expected; so-called rebound effects. These effects occur when an unforeseen consequence in one part of the system is the result of an attempt at problem solving in another part. As ICT, by its very nature, is a network technology, the rebound effects can be significant.

One key challenge from an environmental perspective is that the main driving force today behind the growing use of ICT is not sustainable development, but the urge for short term profit. Increased competitiveness, shorter time to market, increased profit margins and increased market shares; these are the principal reasons for investing in ICT technologies today.

Occasionally these goals may result in a better environment and improve the social situation, but this is relatively rare. By introducing environmental and social considerations from the beginning, many problems could be solved before they even occurred. As no one wants to destroy the environment, create social problems and exacerbate inequity, there should be good opportunities for addressing the existing and potential rebound effects as the new ICT infrastructure is built. The rebound effects that need to be addressed can be divided into three different categories: direct rebound effects, indirect rebound effects and systemic rebound effects.

With ICT penetrating through to new layers of society, many new products will be introduced, and some old products will be altered to include communications capacity.

The potential direct rebound effect of this development could result in a significant increase of new materials as well as increased energy use in different sectors. Two issues are important in this area. First, many of the direct rebound effects can easily be addressed by the introduction of environmental concerns early in the development process. In many cases today, corporate R&D divisions are not even aware of phase out scenarios for toxic substances, and the need for minimal use of energy in all modes and functions. Secondly, the final product must not be the only focus when analysing material use and energy consumption. Even if the product itself does not contain much toxic material or use a lot of energy, the production process might result in toxic waste or be energy intensive.

To solve this problem, all toxic substances should be avoided as far as possible, as should materials that generate toxic material when produced. Furthermore, all energy that is used over the product cycle should come from renewable energy sources. To reduce the material needed for production, products should be designed in modules that can be easily updated and recycled.

It should also be acknowledged that a negative rebound, with effect upon the public image of these products, could be the result if unintelligent solutions are introduced. A situation with higher energy use and more toxic substances released into the environment could create a situation where all ICT-actors would run the risk of being perceived as not taking sustainable development seriously. All serious ICT actors should therefore disclose phase-out strategies for toxic materials and their energy efficiency work.

Indirect rebound effects are not due to the products themselves creating a problem, but to the result of ICT use. These rebound effects are harder to address as they are often beyond the direct control of the ICT producer or user.

The most common example of an indirect rebound effect relates to E-shop-ping. Many times E-shopping "saves "a trip to the shop, with it's attendant pollution and waste of resources, but this environmental gain can easily get lost with an inefficient distribution system. This phenomenon is sometimes called the "Harry Potter rebound effect ",after the event when a new Harry Potter book was sold over the Internet after an intensive marketing campaign. All E-buyers were promised that they would have the book the same day it came out. The result was an extensive transport operation, including airplanes and lorries. Thus, this way of distributing the book was probably one of the worst possible ways from an environmental perspective.

Other indirect rebound effects relate to new cultural and behavioural patterns. A number of virtual contacts with people all over the world, no matter whether professional contacts or personal, could result in an increase in transportation when contacts wish to make the event "real ".On a local scale, specific issues arise when telecommuting becomes more popular. Even if travel to work did decrease, other travels might increase, as telecommuters still need to buy food, obtain child care and make social visits.

When looking at rebound effects, a distinction must be made between temporary transitional indirect rebound effects, and long term systemic rebound effects. In some situations, a higher environmental impact during a short transition period could be necessary to reach a long term sustainable development path. In the same way, a short term improvement can result in a long term systemic rebound effect.

Three of the most serious potential systemic rebounds effects include more transport, more land use and increased consumption. Increased transport is the most obvious systemic rebound effect. If ICT does nothing more than to accelerate the current trend, it will increase the need for the transportation of goods, even if this is done in a slightly more efficient way.

As transport, for the near future, will take place by vehicles using fossil fuel, this is a serious challenge in a situation in which countries that are more affluent must reduce their emissions of carbon dioxide by 60-90 percent. With more control over supplies, less space would be required for storage in warehouses, but on the other hand, it could result in a situation with more goods on the roads, on the way to different shops and factories.

ICT also makes geographical distances less visible, and when using ICT it can be difficult to find out where the product being bought is from, geographically. By using the technology without analysing the long term consequences, incentives for investment in the traditional transport sector can easily be created, resulting in more aeroplanes, lorries and cars, all increasingly polluting the environment and increasing land use.

By using ICT, geographical borders could become less important. This would create incentives for companies and individuals to move to new, still unspoilt areas -and these new settlements would interfere with the small spaces of nature left that humans do not yet dominate. Combined with increased traffic the result would be an even more fragmented environment.

As ICT gives opportunities to consume more and more, the risk of increasing the environmental pressure on our planet and increasing our ecological foot print also expands -along with the risk of creating a culture with no link to nature, and very little time to reflect upon what is important in life.

In order to direct ICT development in a sustainable direction, the different rebound effects must be analysed. This will require new networks, where groups that usually do not have much contact must discuss the challenges. Furthermore, tools must be developed to assess and share information on the different kinds of rebound effects, especially for the systemic rebound effects.

When encouraging the development of a sustainable ICT society, it is tempting to give examples of perfect solutions to today's ecological and environmental problems. Unfortunately, many of these solutions only work under perfect conditions, and their performance under other circumstances can turn out to be counterproductive. There are two main reasons for the exaggeration of ICTs performance.

Firstly, many of those working with ICT are used to talking about efficiency gains of hundreds to thousands of times, and about entirely new ways of solving problems, and understandably want to push the limits. Regrettably, unforeseen, or unlikely, events may be overlooked when the focus is on the highest possible number in a best-case scenario.

Secondly, in order to attract investors and customers, those involved in development and construction of new ICT-enabled products must be heard loudly and clearly in the market. The easiest way to attract attention is to communicate the simplest and most positively staggering numbers -even if these are only valid under certain circumstances.

To strengthen the robustness of the ICT system, three factors should be included in all discussions about new ICT systems and products: possible technological and human errors, feedback mechanisms, and a "cradle to grave " perspective. If all three factors are included, there will be an improved chance of obtaining solutions that resemble dynamic living systems. ICT systems would then be able to handle a vast range of disruptions - however, everything has limits, and when those are reached, the system breaks down.

One good example of where ICTs potential to solve important problems must be dealt with in a responsible manner is product tagging, i.e. providing products with their own identification card. This technology will probably revolutionise the way our economies work, as well as improving environmental protection, making a significant contribution in improving production efficiency and inventory.

At the same time, the introduction of new technologies should not be used as an excuse to delay or halt the phase out of the most toxic substances Keeping this precautionary principle in mind, even a robust ICT-system controlling toxic chemicals should not include chemicals that could be very harmful to the environment.

Another kind of problem relates to the problem when different parts must work together. Often the different parts of a larger system may function effectively, but when errors are encountered, problems such as the "Nimbus-7-blindness "might occur. This name refers to a satellite that was measuring the ozone layer effectively and correctly, but the low values that it was reporting had been covered up by a computer-program designed to discard sudden, large drops in ozone concentrations as "errors ".

It is not hard to design a system that works perfectly in a perfect world, but it is hard to design a system that works well in the context of technological and human error. In every important system, such as systems responsible for energy supply, or toxic measurements, there should therefore be fully redundant back-up systems, as well as planned-out alternative ways of solving the problem, including non-ICT solutions. Instead of trying to build a system that tries to be perfect, in most cases it is better to have a system that is slightly less efficient, but that is robust and can deal with a wide range of errors.

A robust system must be able to handle unforeseen inputs and treat them in a systematic way. As we can anticipate rapid and sudden changes in both ecological systems as well as in society over the coming years, there must be room for unexpected events in all large ICT systems.

In the ICT world, the speed of change is sometimes so rapid that many people forget that many structures will exist for a long time. Whenever sustainable ICT solutions are implemented, no matter their nature, whether application, single product, or the ICT system as a whole, their functions must be optimised instead of maximised. As an ICT response to the precautionary principle, all solutions should be built around the concept of robustness.

Corporations, organisations and political parties are all very enthusiastic about ICT and its possibilities, but judging from the actual results so far, these ideas and thoughts are seldom transformed into concrete action. This lack of results often seems to stem from a lack of focus. Backed only by vague ideas, the process leading up to actual implementation often seems to wind to a halt somewhere before a concrete result has been achieved.

In an attempt to focus attention, this chapter will explore seven strategic areas where action must be taken immediately. These areas cover a wide span of issues and are all important, but in different ways. The areas chosen are, of course, not all that need to be addressed, but are among those that require rapid progress in order to ensure that ICT development will not contribute to the acceleration of the current negative trends, but will instead contribute towards sustainable development. If they are addressed in a successful way, ICTs chances to be used as a positive and useful tool for the future will have been considerably improved.

Importance of ICT Products

The importance of ICT products is due to two basic causes. First, even if ICT products themselves have only a marginal environmental impact, there is a great risk that the political system and mass media will judge the whole sector as environmentally unfriendly if the sector as a whole does not have a clear environmental strategy. Thus, ICTs broader credibility is threatened. Second, the rapid increase and penetration of ICT products can, if no action is taken, result in increased energy demand and bigger quantities of toxic substances. Even if these problems never reach the same magnitude as they have in other sectors, they must not be ignored as they have been so far. This would be easier with clearer targets for energy efficiency and phase out strategies for toxic chemicals used in production.

In order to address the issue of sustainability, the sustainable approach must be integrated throughout the entire life cycle of every new product. Low energy use and the no use of toxic substances should be goals that are encouraged from R&D right through to the final act of recycling a product. In a networked society where hierarchies and responsibilities are often not so simple, combined with rapid technological development, central solutions cannot always be waited upon. Instead, each person involved in interaction with a product should be encouraged to improve sustainability performance.

Many ICT products themselves are very small, but they are numerous. In many cases they have significant ecological baggage, i.e. having created large amounts of waste from the creation of their basic materials through to their production. The cost of solving these problems are, however, small when compared to the overall cost for most ICT products. The ICT sector could therefore play an important leading role when it comes to, energy efficiency, sustainable production and the use of nontoxic materials.

One area where ICT can contribute significantly in the short to medium term relates to the transport of goods. It is clear that ICT can be used to find more optimal transport routes and keep track of large fleets of vehicles.

At first, this would appear to be positive contribution, but it could also result in further investment in a system that is inherently unsustainable. Due care must therefore be taken in order to avoid a situation where investments only result in marginal short term reductions and create an infrastructure that makes it hard to reach the necessary long term solutions.

Physical transport of a product always results in environmental degradation. The biggest environmental challenge today in the field of transport is probably the use of fossil fuel, but even with sustainable energy sources, transportation will come with an environmental cost in terms of energy use and resource consumption. A second inherent problem with physical transport is land use. As soon as goods are moved, there is a renewed demand for space, both for the vehicles to travel on and for the storage of the products. When considering a sustainable transportation system, it is important therefore to always think in terms of service.

This process, along with the encouragement of local production, could set in place a less ecologically damaging economy. Already some sectors have started a process towards a "smart cookie business ",i.e. a business built around the concept of trading and exchanging "recipes ",instead of actual "cookies " thus allowing the product to be made locally. As there will always be a need for the transportation of some goods, there is a clear need to improve the quality of transportation. There is today a rough correlation between the level of environmental impact, and the speed with which goods are transported. This is rarely shown in the price of the product, nor is the environmental impact of the chosen way of transport. By introducing systems where the customer could choose the mode of transportation according to its environmental impact, there would be greater incentives for a sustainable transport system.

One strategic area where more advanced technology already exists, and where there could be a rapid and important shift towards sustainability, is business travel. Not only would a reduction in business travel result in significant environmental gains; but done in the right way it could also contribute to a corporate culture where physical transport would be an option to be avoided if possible.

Increased use of ICT would most certainly be an improvement to today 's economy. Introducing ICT would make the economy more efficient in a number of ways; more accurate estimation of demand, the optimisation of production processes and facilitated updates of products. However, very little indicates that these improvements, sometimes called eco-efficiency, would be sufficient to reduce overall resource and energy use. Efficiency gains so far have been balanced, in most cases, by increased production and consumption by those already consuming a disproportionately large share of the planets resources. If the existing pattern where mankind 's ecological footprint is increasing and the differences in society are dramatically increasing is to change, perspectives must also change.

The first issue to be addressed is the very different economic and social situations on the planet. For the first time in history, a significant proportion of the world 's population is living a life without material scarcity. At the same time, a much larger proportion is still living in poverty. By using the same development model for both systems, many of the negative trends seem to be accelerating instead of reversing.

Solving this challenge requires elaborating solutions for the more affluent parts of the globe to shift their economies from growth economies to quality economies, keeping sustainable development in focus instead of the old economic indicators. This transformation should take into account that the poorer parts of the world need basic goods and services, such as food, transportation, communication, medicine and housing. By shifting the research and production patterns in the more developed economies, a situation would be created which would facilitate a jump forward for the poor countries, over the resource-intensive industrial society, and straight into a post-industrial society with low environmental impact.

The energy system is just one example where most rich countries today have a centralised large-scale system that is designed to deal with very large fluctuations. In a situation with a small-scale decentralised system, where it is possible to communicate between producer and consumer, there is no need to build the same kind of overcapacity, nor would it necessarily have to be based on fossil fuels.

From the customers ' perspective, ICT could be used to find the product that is most environmentally friendly for the specific situation. This of course requires that companies make available information about the environmental performance of their products on the Internet. As the amount of information freely available continues to increase, there will be a need for tools that help to identify sustainable solutions, for example "intelligent agents ";programs that help to search for specific information on the Internet. By introducing environmental and social parameters, these agents could help users to find products and producers that supply sustainable solutions to different needs. If these agents could be tailor made to fit different needs, they could play an important part in increasing the level of sustainable development.

Although many new technical solutions will be created in the future, the most important development from a sustainable perceptive would be if ICT could contribute to a society that focused less on people as consumers, and more on their role as citizens. ICT-systems should therefore encourage the distribution of free information, whilst being developed to leave room for dreams and visions. Looking ahead, many of today 's trends show that the exploitation of natural areas will continue. Resources required for the poor of the world, growing urban sprawl, increased transport, and the larger ecological footprints of more affluent societies all contribute to a situation where a minimal part of Nature is beyond immediate danger of exploitation. In order to address this issue a multi-prong strategy is required, wherein ICT could play a significant role. Transportation and consumption have already been discussed, but there are many more gains that can be made in the field of sustainable land use.

First, ICT can help monitor land use in a more efficient manner than is currently the standard. Satellites and probes in remote areas can help to understand and identify different threats, such as illegal cutting of forests. Geographical Information Systems (GIS) may also be used to optimise land use in different areas.

Second, ICT can be used to communicate not only the threats to, but also the beauty of untouched areas. New technologies could be developed that would make it possible to follow life in remote areas from anywhere on the planet, which would improve personal identification with Nature and its values, such as those that exist in remote places like Antarctica, the coral reefs and the untouched rainforests.

ICT can also be used for more direct educational purposes, such as calculating and communicating the footprints left by various lifestyles in different parts of the world. This helps to determine different ways of reducing society 's ecological footprints, and aids the realisation that high quality life can be combined with a small footprint. With ICT, strategies to align local, regional, national and international conservation work could also be further developed, which would make all of these far more effective on a global scale.

With ICT and genetically modified organisms (GMOs) already available, difficult ethical, environmental and economic questions beg to be discussed. Much indicates that ethical questions regarding new technologies will be even more important in the years to come, as there will probably be new breakthroughs in areas such as biotechnology, nanotechnology, robotics and quantum computing.

If these technologies, and especially the combination of these technologies, are to be used in a responsible way, and if technological development is to contribute solving at least some of the challenges faced today, there is a clear need to approach the issue in a strategic way.

Today, whilst many products are developed only for the richest parts of society, this is partly due to the type of economic structures, including business models that have been created over time. These structures are often built around the idea of a large-scale production system, where the market consists only of a high or medium-income population. This system therefore tends to exclude many parts of the worlds population and ecology that really need the help of the newest technologies.

In order to direct ICT and broader technological development in a sustainable direction, independent agencies should be created on both the national and international level to evaluate emerging technologies. One way to address this issue would be to develop an International Convention on New Technologies, to assess the societal and political implications of emerging technologies before their commercial release.

Today a digital divide, both within and between countries, is growing. This divide is a serious issue, as it tends to increase already existing gaps, making the poor on this planet even more isolated than before. At the same time, most new ICT-technologies are built around new principles such as decentralisation and flexibility, all principles that make leapfrogging over stages of development easier.

Two things need to be taken into account when talking about the divide between those who have the technological resources, tools and the knowledge to generate and distribute information, and those who do not.

First, the digital divide must be addressed together with the wider, and more classical economical divides. Far too often, attempts to bridge the digital divide are presented either as being in opposition to other development goals, or as the single solution to all problems.

Neither of these approaches is particularly constructive. To address this challenge, there must be a change in the methodology for addressing basic needs, acknowledging that it will be impossible for a purely commercial perspective to be used to close the digital divide.

Secondly, the cultural gap must also be bridged where the commercial values from one kind of culture dominate the design and development of large parts of the ICT system. There is an urgent need to develop strategies for the creation of cultural space and education for groups, so that the ICT system becomes a system built around diversity, wherein all different groups have their needs fulfilled.

3

Development of E-Commerce

The measurement of people's access to the Internet and the use they make of it remains far from perfect. The problem is particularly acute when it comes to quantitative information about e-commerce in developing countries, where internationally comparable, freely accessible figures are especially scarce. Nevertheless, even if discrepancies in terms of absolute levels exist even among the most reliable sources, a trend towards a rapid increase in the relevant magnitudes is apparent. The Internet continues to grow rapidly

According to the International Telecommunication Union (ITU), the number of Internet users worldwide stood at 500 million people at the end of 2001. This represents 115 million more than at the end of 2000 (or about a 30 per cent increase). The ITU forecasts that at the end of 2002 the global number of Internet users will have grown to 655 million, which would represent a yearly rate of growth of around 31 per cent. In other words, more than 150 million people, roughly the equivalent of a country like the Russian Federation, or 2.5

per cent of the world's population, would be joining the numbers of Internet users every year.Owing to differences in definitions and methodologies, other sources provide slightly different figures; table 1 provides an overview of various estimates of Internet demographics at the end of 2001 and forecasts for 2002. A figure of 500 million current Internet users around the world would therefore seem to be a safe estimate.

Table 1

Estimates of Internet users worldwide (millions)

Source	2001	2002
ITU	500.07	655 (forecast)
Nielsen//NetRatings	498.20	
IDC	497.70	
Nua.com	527.57	580.78 (May)

Table 2 uses ITU figures for 2000 and 2001 to show the geographical distribution of the growth in the Internet population:

Table 2

Internet users (thousands), 2000 -2001, by region

Region	2001	2000	Increase	% change
Africa	6 738	4 601	2 137	46.4
South Africa	3 068	2 400	668	27.8
Egypt	600	450	150	33.3
Kenya	500	200	300	150.0
Morocco	400	200	200	100.0
Tunisia	400	250	150	60.0
Others	1 770	1 101	669	60.8
Latin America **& Caribbean**	26 320	19 331	6 989	36.2
Brazil	8 000	5 000	3 000	60.0
México	3 636	2 712	923	34.0
Chile	3 102	2 537	565	22.3
Argentina	3 000	2 500	500	20.0

Peru	3 000	2 500	500	20.0
Venezuela	1 300	950	350	36.8
Colombia	1 154	878	276	31.4
Others	3 128	2 253	875	38.8
North America	156 323	136 700	19 623	14.4
United States	142 823	124 000	18 823	15.2
Canada	13 500	12 700	800	6.3
Asia	157 779	108 231	49 547	45.8
Japan	57 900	37 200	20 700	55.6
China	33 700	22 500	11 200	49.8
Republic of Korea	24 380	19 040	5 340	28.0
Taiwan Province of China	7 820	6 260	1 560	24.9
India	7 000	5 500	1 500	27.3
Others	26 979	17 731	9 247	52.2
Europe	144 410	108 339	36 071	33.3
Germany	30 000	24 000	6 000	25.0
United Kingdom	24 000	18 000	6 000	33.3
Italy	16 000	13 200	2 800	21.2
France	15 653	8 500	7 153	84.2
Spain	7 388	5 387	2 000	37.1
Netherlands	5 300	3 900	1 400	35.9
Sweden	4 600	4 048	552	13.6
Russian Federation	4 300	3 100	1 200	38.7
Poland	3 800	2 800	1 000	35.7
Others	33 369	25 403	7 966	31.4
Oceania	8 505	7 635	870	11.4
Australia	7 200	6 600	600	9.1
New Zealand	1 092	830	262	31.6
Others	213	205	8	3.9
World	500 074	384 837	115 237	29.9

The data show that a growing share of new Internet users are in developing countries. Overall, developing countries accounted for almost one third of new Internet users worldwide in 2001. In the most developed markets penetration is nearing saturation levels as the numbers of those who do not plan to get Internet access in the near future seem to have stabilized.

Therefore, the growth in the share of developing countries will continue. Already Asia, excluding Japan and the Republic of Korea, added almost 21 million new users to the Internet in 2001, more than North America. Recent data from sources other than ITU would put the number of Internet users in China at 56.6 million, thus making China the second largest Internet population in the world in absolute numbers.

In spite of the encouraging increase in the number of users, penetration rates in most developing countries remain very low. On the basis of ITU estimates, the percentage of the world's population using the Internet at the end of 2001 should have been around 8 per cent, that is 30 per cent higher than the 6.4 per cent that the ITU calculated at the end of 2000, but still far below the 50 per cent and above penetration rates in the most advanced countries.

The fact that more and more people are using the Internet, which is a prerequisite for the expansion of e-commerce, is not necessarily an indication of the existence of such expansion or of its pace.

Some estimates of the numbers of Internet users count anyone (including, for instance, children) who has had access to the Internet in the previous 30 days. A much higher frequency of access is necessary in order to acquire the familiarity and generate the confidence that are needed in order to become an e-commerce practitioner. Particularly in the case of those engaged in business-to-business (B2B) e-commerce, the order of magnitude of their use of the Internet cannot be of some hours per month, but of hours per day.

Indeed, when asked about the use they make of the Internet, people rarely mention e-commerce as a frequent online activity. In a survey of 12 countries, e-mail was the only Internet activity in which more than 50 per cent of respondents in every country surveyed had been engaged in the previous six months. It is safe to assume that in developing countries the proportion of Internet users who are also e-commerce practitioners is lower than average, owing of course to lower per capita incomes but also to other well-known factors such as low credit card usage, lack of relevant products or services or poor logistics and fulfilment services.

It seems that the gap between developed and developing countries in terms of access to and use of the Internet is smaller than the one in terms of e-commerce volumes. The differences between forecasts are remarkable. However, while the estimates and forecasts of the absolute levels of e-commerce for a given year can vary by a maximum factor of 2.8 times, the expected rates of growth move in a narrower band, with the highest value 17 percentage points above the lowest. Compounded even over a relatively short span of time, such differences in growth rates yield massive differences in absolute figures, but all three of them represent extremely rapid increases in global e-commerce volumes.

Job opportunities for women

E-commerce offers some attractive possibilities for small business owners in the developing countries' business-to-consumer (B2C) or retail sector, many of the enterprises in which are owned by women. Numerous examples have been cited as digital opportunities for women entrepreneurs along the models of telecentres in Senegal and Morocco, phone shops in Ghana, Internet cafes or kiosks in Thailand and Malaysia, and the Grameen Phone in Bangladesh. The latter has been cited as a successful example of women entrepreneurship, where financing from the Grameen Bank allows women to buy cellphones and provide mobile pay phone services in their shops or local markets at a mutually agreed mark-up with Grameen Telecom.

Aside from telephony services, women's handicrafts could also be developed using B2C, although difficulties in terms of marketing and management skills, and supply and delivery logistics need to be addressed. A number of success stories concerning B2C endeavours are to be found in South Asia, Latin America, Africa and the Middle East.

In India, an e-marketplace called IndiaShop eliminated the middlemen in the selling of saris. One woman allegedly sold a silk sari she tailored for $ 1,100, a price that is way above an average Indian's annual income.

In Peru, a nationwide network of housewives called Tortasperu, which is involved in baking confectioneries sold over the Internet, showcased lucrative work for women at home taking care of children yet providing the country with much needed foreign exchange. Ethiopia has opened a gift shop that sells, using the Internet, traditional Ethiopian costumes, food items and spices produced by women.

Finally, handmade products made by women artisans in Egypt, Jordan, Lebanon, Morocco and Tunisia are sold through a virtual shop called Elsouk. These digital opportunities are particularly significant for women in Asia, considering that women head 35 per cent of small and medium-sized enterprises (SMEs). It has been reported that in China women initiate about 25 percent of new business start-ups and in Japan four out of five small business owners are women.

The main advantage of the Web for small home-based businesses is the information and networking opportunities that would make these endeavours profitable rather than marginal. Despite these success stories in e-retailing, it will be necessary to evaluate carefully in which segments of e-commerce women's opportunities lie. Women's prospects depend primarily on the trading strength of the countries concerned.

In many cases, the use of the Internet is confined to advertising, ordering and possibly collecting payments; hence women have to develop strategies to build consumers' confidence in the quality of their goods. The limited evidence available so far shows that some women have also found a market niche in the buying and selling of information rather than tangible goods. In addition to the example of the Grameen Phone cited earlier, women in India and Malaysia use online delivery of their services as freelance journalists to newspapers and other publishers.

More promising opportunities for women lie in the B2B segment of e-commerce. The advances in computer and communication technologies have made it possible to transfer digitized data online when there is an adequate supply of infrastructure and bandwidth. Through the use of networking technologies, large amounts of information can be transported at very low cost from the companies' core offices to satellite or subcontracting units. This possibility has led companies to externalize and decentralize non-core sections of business operations to distant and often cheaper locations. The targeted sites are usually the ones that offer the promises of a cheap, skilled computer-and English-literate workforce. This phenomenon explains why companies in OECD countries outsource service operations to countries such as India or Malaysia. The International Data Corporation (IDC) estimated that spending on IT outsourcing had reached $ 56 billion in 2000 and would exceed $ 100 billion by 2005. There has been some evidence of companies in developing countries outsourcing operations within the country as well as to other developing countries where wages are even cheaper. Some of the Indian companies, for example, look towards Nepal for the requisite workforce at times of peak demand, particularly from abroad.

In Malaysia, subcontracting or outsourcing takes place primarily within national boundaries. There is a relationship between the availability of a skilled, English-speaking female workforce and where outsourcing normally happens. From this, one can also propose the hypothesis of the existence of a relationship between the availability of a skilled female workforce and foreign direct investment in information processing work in the developing countries.

The software services sector in countries such as India and the Philippines could support this hypothesis. The salary differences between the United States and India, or the Philippines, for similar skills are considerable. Yet these differences cannot fully explain the absence of relocation of software services to countries such as Bangladesh or Uganda where salaries are even lower. In addition to the requisite skills, the success of replicating the experience of India or Philippines depends on creating the right policy framework. Software and IT-enabled services could be export-oriented as in the case of India and the Philippines; they could also be domestically oriented as is in the case of Malaysia, China and Brazil.

The global expansion of those services has broadened the job prospects of women in new areas. The limited statistics that we have so far indicate that women in some of the Asian and Latin American countries occupy more than 20 per cent of professional jobs in software services.

Recent research and projections have indicated that the prospects for women lie more in the IT-enabled services than in software services. The worldwide demand for IT-enabled services or business process outsourcing (BPO) is expected to grow at a dramatic rate in the coming decade, reaching $ 611.4 billion by the year 2005. India hopes to capture a large share of this newly created market. With revenues of $ 870 million from IT-enabled services in 2000-2001 and an annual growth rate of 66 per cent, it currently has the potential to address 38 per cent of that market.

Again, there are no gender-disagregated statistics on employment arising out of these outsourced IT-enabled services from the developing world. According to the Deputy Director of the Confederation of Indian Industries (CII), in India at least 40 per cent of these newly created jobs are given to, and taken by, women.

Remote services or IT-enabled services largely consist in the relocation of back-office operations. One has to be cautious about the future, however, given that there are various types of back-office services requiring different levels of skills from women and men.

The increasing trend towards outsourcing by major American and European corporations entails jobs ranging from those at the lower end of the skills level where women are mostly employed, such as data entry and data capture, to those at the higher end such as software programming, geographical information systems (GIS) and systems analysis. There is a discernible trend towards hiring women for operations that require less complex skills.

For the benefit of the women and for augmenting or retaining the competitive advantage of countries, policy makers need to ensure that women receive the same opportunities and encouragement to acquire skills that could equip them for more complex and specialized jobs.

The outsourcing or externalizing of business processes to distant units within or across the national boundary could range from satellite offices, such as call centres, to homes of employees or vendors or to offices of customers or clients.

With the computer and a modem, a woman can be connected to the head office and can perform her professional work from a distant site such as a neighbourhood centre or her own home. This is possible as long as her work involves storing, processing, retrieving and delivering digitized information. This new mode of working is known as teleworking and has received much attention, particularly in the context of women's career prospects. The use of ICT in itself can, in theory, offer a solution that is attractive both to women and to the corporate sector interested in retaining skilled women employees.

"Tele" implies distance and teleworking refers to ICT-mediated distant work. The term covers both home-based work or telecommuting and institution-based work as carried out in call centres, neighbourhood centres or satellite offices. Home-based teleworking could, in theory, enhance the participation of women in the digital economy as it allows a certain flexibility in both the timing and location of work. Women with caring responsibilities at home welcome this flexibility, but not without reservation. Whereas some women appreciate the opportunities that teleworking brings, the majority fear that the home-based work will deprive them of the status of working women and hinder their professional or business efficiency.

Surveys of home-based teleworking carried out in Mumbai and Kuala Lumpur revealed that women had a preference for institution-based teleworking as in call centres (home-based teleworking accounted for only 1.0 and 0.35 per cent respectively). According to Ng and Khoo, in Malaysia, "interviews with women's groups indicated that the (institution-based) centres, commercial and state sponsored, may be the ideal site for externalised work that will allow women (and men) to combine work with collective childcare facilities; enable women (and men) with peer groups and thus allow them to acquire and improve their tacit skills; and provide facilities for state and corporate sector supported vocational training in the field of computer literacy".

Managerial concerns may also explain the low prevalence of home-based teleworking in India and Malaysia. In a survey of management perception of teleworking in Malaysia, most respondents reported that in Malaysian culture face-to-face interaction was essential. In India too, research revealed a cautious attitude on the part of management towards home-based teleworking. In the financial sector, for example, companies find it prudent to outsource work to call centres rather than to teleworkers.

In institution-based teleworking it is easy to monitor and supervise employees in the traditional way, whereas widespread implementation of home-based teleworking will require a fundamental shift in the culture of management from direct supervision to a basis of trust. For self-employed and freelance workers, home-based teleworking will involve self-management and time management skills. It is important for women to acquire these skills in order to avoid being distracted by household chores or over working while teleworking from home.

There is no uniformity in the preference for types of telework among women in the developing countries. Age and stage of life are key factors in moulding women's choice regarding the type of telework. In Mumbai, while young women work in call centres or offices of foreign airline companies in the export processing zones, older women, with young children, opt for and receive home-based telework.

Companies such as Datamatics - a rapidly growing software house - receive assignments from their international clients. In turn, they pass these to women teleworkers who work from their homes, mostly online and with their own computers. These home-based teleworkers comprise a wide range of women: housewives, doctors, lawyers and chartered accountants.

All that they have in common is that they had to give up regular employment at some stage for the sake of their families. Teleworking gives them a welcome and much-needed opportunity to be in touch with the world of work. Yet it is difficult to ensure that these women can progress, with adequate access to training and childcare, to high value-added jobs. The experience of Malaysia is similar. "The case studies in software, as well as in printing and publishing, indicate that some women often opt for and find satisfaction in home-based work, either as freelancer or as employees. This happens in a particular phase of their life cycle, especially when there are inadequate child care facilities". The provision of childcare thus remains a key issue in recruiting, retaining and retraining women in the new economy, as it was in the old economy.

In some countries, such as India, Malaysia, the Philippines and Jamaica, call centres have already proved to be a success in allowing women to participate in the digital economy. The proportion of women employed by call centres varies from 40-70 per cent. They tend to be between 20 and 25 years of age and in most cases this is their first job. In view of the projected growth of these call centres, women are likely to benefit at least numerically from this segment of e-commerce.

There are risks of a reduction in demand for outsourcing call centre services to developing countries resulting from the improvement of voice recognition by computers. In addition, changes in technology may alter the volume and the nature of call centre service provision. Instead of providing a central base for teleworking, call centre services may be provided virtually, supported by fast data communication linkages among a network of home-based teleworkers. Again, the deployment of web-based technologies may reduce the market for call centre service provision.

In banking, for example, customers may conduct their own transactions. In this new environment, instead of focusing on a single task, institutions such as call centres or satellite offices will be engaged in multidimensional tasks. Women therefore need to have access to appropriate training and lifelong education in order to retain their share in this changing market. Second, there is a prospect of "burn out" syndrome.

One reason given was the highly competitive environment as incentives are given to top performers in call success rates (for example, in debt collection efforts), implying reprimands and threats of dismissals for low success rates. These employees have to deal most civilly with their recipients many of whom tend to be abusive or even hysterical.

While the call centre industry has the ability to provide young women with the means of entry into the banking sector, the danger lies with it being a dead-end job, with limited career promotion prospects." For women, call centres located on the outskirts of cities reduce the need to commute; for the management they offer the possibility of adequate supervision for ensuring quality control.

ICT and e-commerce can create a number of promising economic opportunities for women in developing countries. They have also pointed to the various obstacles that need to be addressed in order to enhance women's participation in the information economy. One of the most important impediments to women's engaging in ICT-enabled employment possibilities Why is there such an uneven distribution of male and female employees across ICT-related occupations and what could be done to address this? The training policies in developing countries are in theory gender-neutral.

In practice, however, they are often geared to the life cycle and aspirations of men. Women, particularly of child-bearing age, find it difficult to cope with the training given either by employers or by private sector institutions. The dropout rate for women even in the high-skilled software services sector has been alarming, even in areas where there is a need for trained personnel.

The major ICT markets are now faced with a serious shortage of IT skills. IDC estimated a total of 3.7 million IT jobs in 2000 (excluding people who used some IT expertise in their main functions). In relates to skills and training and will be considered in this section. Assessing the parity between women and men in the digital economy is a complex task.

In order to enhance women's participation in e-commerce at all levels, it is important to identify areas of expertise needed by the corporate sector for e-commerce in developing countries. This is particularly so as ICT-related trade in services has led to a dichotomy between ICT-focused and business-focused activities. For the purpose of monitoring and facilitating women's entry into key occupations, it could useful to consider the various core activities for conducting e-commerce.

IDC divides ICT services industries into two categories:

(a) IT activities primarily targeting information systems and technology-enabled processes; and

(b) Business activities primarily targeting business processes along the value chain (e.g. primary activities such as manufacturing, marketing and sales and services; and support activities such as procurement and logistics, human resource management, and research and development).

The potential implications for women of this distinction between information technology activities and business activities could be enormous. Many business activities and corporate functions, especially back-office support operations such as typing, scheduling, filing or communications, are now becoming ICT-based and it is women in many, if not all, corporate entities who carry out these functions. Thus, women should learn these required ICT skills to prevent bottlenecks from occurring in the corporate infrastructure. In addition, this framework could be used for benchmarking women's progress, or the lack of it, in key areas of activities related to e-commerce.

Given the scenario of a prevailing IT skills shortage and the increasing trend towards business activities and corporate functions becoming IT-based, another manifestation of the gender digital divide is the lack of adequate representation of women in the higher echelons of IT-related jobs. Few women are actual producers of information technology as Internet content providers, web designers, software programmers or computer troubleshooters.

In the United States, females comprise a minority in mid to upper-level IT-related jobs, notwithstanding the fact that 50 per cent of Internet users in the country are women. For instance, only 9 per cent of engineers, 28.5 per cent of computer programmers and 26.9 per cent of systems analysts in the United States are females. Women, however, reportedly constitute the majority (85 per cent) of data entry workers. Moreover, there are gender disparities in the salaries between men and women in IT in the United States. According to Taggart and O'Gara, women in IT career jobs earn 67 per cent of what their male counterparts earn. It is to be expected that this disparity would be much wider in developing countries.

In contrast, the networking or programming courses are predominantly attended by their male counterparts, who would thus obviously be equipped for higher-paying jobs and more remunerative IT career paths. The authors suggest therefore that trends in access to and use of IT are not sufficient indicators for the equitable participation of women in the information society. Instead, what should be looked at is how women use the Internet and what skills they are equipped with, as these would determine their role in and contribution to the digital economy. In order to meet the impending skill shortages in critical areas, women must therefore be prepared for careers at all levels of the ICT sector, from data entry to software design, network management and IT entrepreneurship. In considering how ICTs and the Internet could benefit women economically and socially, policy-makers should think beyond women selling their crafts via the web, to women selling their skills as website designers, network managers or IT services consultants.

Women in developing countries do not yet find it easy to obtain suitable jobs or income-generating work in the fields of network management, web design or software development, because they are not equipped with the necessary skills. The explanation does not necessarily lie in discrimination against women in centres of education and training in developing countries.

In developing as well as in developed countries, there are difficulties in attracting and retaining women in ICT training and education. An example used by Taggart and O'Gara from the experience of Cisco's international

Networking Academy Program (CNAP) provides some answers to why women's participation in IT training has been minimal . Cisco Networking Academy Program (CNAP) is an international training program that teaches students to design, build, and maintain computer networks. The CNAP curriculum is offered in over 70 countries and taught through web-based modules facilitated by on-site instructors in secondary schools, technical colleges, universities, and non-governmental organizations. Minimum education requirements are an eighth grade reading and math level.

Students and instructors in Cisco's program voice a common message that once women are in the programme, they excel, and in fact perform better than male students.

In the Philippines, where employment and career prospects are more limited than in the United Kingdom, opportunities for overseas work depict a higher proportion of women graduating in ICT. While women lag behind their male counterparts in ICT enrolment, they are ahead of males in terms of

Apart from skills and training, there are a number of other constraints that prevent women from fully engaging in the opportunities created by the digital economy. These obstructing factors, described below, are essentially access to Internet technologies, availability of credit or financing, the language of the Internet and other social and cultural barriers.

Many researchers and policy makers have expressed concern that inequality in access to Internet technology will increase the existing polarity between countries as well as between groups within a country. In such discussions on the digital divide, gender issues have received attention. The ITU gave a timely warning on impending cyber sex discrimination, since it viewed cyberspace as a predominantly male area where the technical and managerial roles are assumed by men.

Its World Telecommunication Development Report 2002 (WTDR) portrays a different and more optimistic future. The spread of very small aperture terminal (VSAT) technology and mobile telephony has considerably narrowed the teledensity gap between the developed and developing world. Also, the third-generation mobile telephone promises to bring networking technology in a cost-effective way to women who are not privileged, even in the rural areas. Access to infrastructure alone, in the absence of access to market and skills, will not enhance participation in e-commerce.

Human resource development issues that focus on technical and marketing skills should perhaps feature as prominently as infrastructure in a policy framework. The cost of infrastructure, however, is likely to remain a major issue for both women and men, particularly in the poorer countries. In Bangladesh, for example, the cost of a computer equals nearly two years' salary for a professional person, and a modem costs more than a cow.

The collective use of telephone and Internet facilities to some extent helps, or might help, traditionally disadvantaged groups, such as women, to overcome the challenges of infrastructure constraints. The use of cyberkiosks and Internet cafes are examples of collective use facilities that come from the market-oriented private sector. Telecentres present possibilities of collective use with subsidies and support from donor agencies and the public sector.

Concerns about bandwidth are often overlooked in the discussion of collective use. To conduct e-commerce in a sustainable and efficient way, it is not enough to have connectivity - the right amount of bandwidth is also needed. Developing countries generally lag behind the developed ones in a dramatic way in terms of access to bandwidth.

According to the ITU, there is an uneven distribution of bandwidths among countries - for example, the 400,000 citizens of Luxembourg between them have more international Internet bandwidth than Africa's 760 million citizens. Given their position in the economy and in society in poorer parts of the world, it is likely that women more than men will have problems in having access to adequate bandwidth necessary for conducting e-commerce. This is an issue that policy makers should be concerned with.

Disagregation of Internet usage by gender is difficult to obtain, especially from developing countries, and if available the data are not very reliable and comparable. However, even if the figures are not reliable, the numbers of women Internet users are very likely to be small in developing countries, considering that statistics that are not even disagregated by gender show already a very small or insignificant proportion of Internet access for the entire population.

Home access to the Internet in many developing countries is a rare phenomenon. Unlikely to have computers at home, most women in developing countries also cannot afford to use public access sites. User fees charged for Internet access at public venues may not be affordable for women, who are generally less able than men to pay fees (averaging $1 to $3 an hour).

When women do have access in developing countries, it is usually in the workplace. This creates a dichotomy between the use of ICT by women as tools of production (e.g. routine office work, data entry, programming) and tools of communication (e.g. creation and exchange of information). As to the latter, women working for non-governmental organizations have used the Internet mainly for political advocacy to protect women's rights and women's causes ranging from domestic violence issues to sexual slavery.

Apart from access to infrastructure and education (skills), lack of capital is the third key obstacle facing women (especially women entrepreneurs) wishing to engage in e-commerce and e-business. To start up ICT-enabled businesses or to employ ICT tools to enhance existing businesses, women will need capital from special financial institutions in developing countries that lend specifically to women entrepreneurs who have no collateral, and who work mostly in the informal sector. The most likely source of the necessary financial capital could be microcredit schemes that specifically target women because of high take-up and repayment experiences and social dividends reaped from lending to them. In this sense, ICT-enabled businesses are no different from other traditional microenterprises in which women in developing countries are engaged. They both involve light-based manufacturing, trade, or service activities; employ about five people or less, mostly family members; have low barriers to market entry; are home-based; and require less professional experience and knowledge than those of their male partners. The only differentiating factor is the use of new technologies.

The microfinance or microcredit programmes are aimed at empowering women beyond just the setting up or expansion of microenterprises. Specifically, microcredit schemes increase women's income levels and their economic independence, enhance their autonomy over household decisions about expenditures, promote positive attitudes to women's social and political roles in communities, and provide them with information and support networks to protect their individual and collective interests at the local and macro levels.

In the case of ICT-enabled businesses, the Grameen Phone Project in Bangladesh described in section B stands out as a best practice model combining lending to women's microenterprises with literacy training and skills development. As described by Hafkin and Taggart, among the two million borrowers of the Grameen Bank, who received wireless phones as an in-kind loan to village phone operators, 75 per cent are women. The operators resell the mobile phone service to fellow villagers, earning an average annual income of $300 as against the national average per capita income of $286. About 90 per cent of the women operators are married and have no formal education. The phone business can be managed simultaneously with another business or while doing household chores.

The major advantages of this type of ICT-enabled enterprise are the minimal educational requirements (just some basic mechanical aptitude), and the small capital needed, enough to be supported by microcredit schemes. There are positive externalities also in accelerating rural development where telecommunication density is sparse.

Another successful example of ICT-enabling business with a microfinancing component is the use of smart cards by Indian women milk collectors in Rajasthan. The smart cards were used to record the quality, fat content and sales of milk to distributors and served as their bankbook, thereby empowering them to make spending decisions and increasing their profits while eliminating the middlemen (called dhudhwala).

The dominance of English as the language of the Internet represents a serious problem for the majority of the world's population, which does not speak English. Women without access to formal schooling that allows them to learn foreign languages are again marginalized, but so are men in countries or regions where English is not "the" language, such as Latin America, the Middle East, French-speaking Africa and Eastern Europe.

Even where women do have equal access to formal schooling, they may need to receive additional training in foreign language skills, for which time and resources will be scarce. While the predominance of English is a threat to the social inclusion of non-English-speaking women in the digital economy, the increasing trend towards multilingual content provides a digital opportunity in terms of language translation in software development and in web design in native languages.

Many of the previously discussed factors affecting women's participation in the information economy are directly linked to the roles and positions of women in society and the family. In low-income families, parents tend to give priority to the education of boys rather than girls. Also, women often have less control over family income (in particular if men are the main income earners), which makes it more difficult for them to pursue (fee-based) training in IT-related fields or spend family income on ICT access and use. Prevailing gender stereotypes discourage girls from pursuing science, technology or engineering careers in many developing countries, especially in Africa, where the numbers of female students in these fields are particularly low.

In some cultures, women's presence in public is restricted. Women may not be able to travel to undergo training or attend courses by male teachers, while at the same time few female teachers in the IT and engineering fields may be available. Also, women may not be allowed to use public Internet access centres or telecentres and hence will depend more heavily on home-based access. Lack of interaction with the public also restricts women's opportunities to practise foreign language skills. Even in societies where women's presence in public is not restricted, the cur-remote services, this could work well for women wishing to combine household responsibilities with income-earning activities.

Since the top two outsourcing markets - the United States and the United Kingdom- are both English-speaking, those developing countries that would want to tap those markets would have to learn English. English proficiency has been mentioned by outsourcing companies as one of the key requirements. This gives rise to some policy implications for improving the schooling and literacy of women where a second language -English - should be learned.

Improving women's access to Internet technologies requires extensive infrastructure building of basic telecommunications (including wireless and satellite) in rural and peri-urban areas, which are currently underserved in many developing countries. This should involve common facilities such as telecentres and phone shops that offer public Internet services and are located in venues which women frequent, such as markets, churches, health clinics, schools and post offices.

Microcredit programmes should target the poorest, marginalized women, improving delivery mechanisms that involve men so as to increase their perception of the intervention as supplementing family income instead of being a threat to status. Women should be allowed greater control over their incomes and be given greater powers of decision about family expenditures. A perhaps more radical implication would be the empowerment of women by allowing them titles to conjugal assets so that they could eventually be able to qualify for financing from the formal financial sector.

In the area of job creation, policy makers need to promote IT-enabled employment such as teleworking. In developing countries institution-based teleworking generally appears to be a more attractive option than home-based teleworking, both for working mothers with young children and for management. For relatively highly skilled women, for example in software programming and the media, home-based teleworking, at certain stages of their lives, could provide a solution to problems of combining childcare responsibilities with those of ICT-related professions.

But even for these women, policy makers need to ensure better provision of childcare facilities so that they do not settle for home-based and/or less challenging occupations because there is little choice. In other words, a policy framework needs to take into account the complexities of women's aspirations and life cycles with regard to enhancing their participation in all segments of e-commerce.

Women in small-scale business face additional hurdles as regards making use of ICT either for marketing or for advertising because of their limited access to market information, finance, assets and infrastructure. This is where the real challenge lies for policy makers in their efforts to bridge the (gender) digital divide and include the poorest segments of the population.

E-business developments

The IT industry provides essential instruments that make e-business possible, including not only computer hardware and software but also fixed telephones, mobile telephones, telecommunication equipment and wireless transmission equipment. The availability of IT equipment goes hand in hand with Internet connectivity and is therefore clearly a prerequisite for e-business. Even though e-business impinges on IT goods, this does not necessarily imply that having a local IT producing industry would be an advantage for the local business sector when it moves into e-business.

However, when the business sector starts adopting new information and communications technologies in its operations, it relies heavily on local or locally available IT expertise in order to fully realize all the efficiency gains that the Internet makes possible at the level of a single firm as well as at the level of the industry and of the country's economy as a whole. In this connection, the existence of a local IT sector or of investment from IT multinationals might contribute to the takeoff of e-business in developing countries if it promotes IT awareness and culture in the local business sector, if it advances the IT competencies of the workforce and if it brings the technology closer to the local business community. Although reliable data on the IT industry are hard to find, it is safe to say that IT is one of the world's largest industries. According to one estimate, "worldwide IT spending has reached almost $988 billion and is expected to increase at a compound annual growth rate (CAGR) of 9.4 per cent from 2001 to 2006 to reach $1.5 trillion".

The IT industry, having suffered a setback in 2001 due to the economic recession and the effects of the tragic events of 11 September, might experience a modest recovery in 2002. Growth should then pick up again in 2003. The IT sector was the subject of intense negotiations during the Uruguay Round and remains so today. In December 1996, at the first WTO Ministerial Conference held in Singapore 54 WTO Member States signed the Information Technology Agreement Its two most important characteristics are that:

— It was signed as a separate document, and is therefore not a part of the "Single Undertaking': for this reason, participation in the Agreement is not compulsory for WTO member countries and for countries that are in the process of accession to the WTO;

— It is a tariff-cutting mechanism that obliges its members to cut tariffs of all products covered to zero.

Trade in IT products grew tremendously over the last decade and was worth over $ 900 billion in 2000. In particular, exports of IT products from developing countries grew at a compound annual growth rate (CAGR) of 23.5 per cent over the last decade, while exports from developed countries grew at a CAGR of 10.8 per cent. By comparison, total world exports grew by 6 per cent over the same period. As a consequence, the share of developing countries and economies in transition in IT exports grew from 15.6 per cent of exports in 1990 to 35.5 per cent in 2000.

It is also worth noting that IT exports represent a higher share in the exports of developing countries than in those of developed countries. In fact, IT exports grew from 12 per cent of total developing countries' exports in 1990 to 22 per cent of their total exports in 2000, while for developed countries the share was respectively 10 per cent in 1990 and 14 per cent in 2000. This phenomenon was a result of transnational corporations strategies for locating hardware production in emerging markets, as well as of developing countries' efforts to develop local IT production capacities which resulted in important outsourcing of IT production to those countries.

The main sub-sectors within the IT industry were semiconductors, electronic data processing (EDP), office equipment (OE), telecommunications equipment, components and miscellaneous goods. The two largest of these - accounting for almost 60 per cent of IT exports - were EDP and semiconductors.

EDP was the largest sub-sector, with 29 per cent of total IT exports in 2000. This segment includes personal computers, mainframe computers and peripherals such as keyboards, printers, monitors, cables and modems. Storage units, for example hard drives but also CDs and diskettes, are also included in this category. It is interesting to note that trade in EDP includes trade in packaged software, although this is not specifically mentioned. This happens for two sets of reasons: on the one hand, a large proportion of internationally traded software is installed in new computer devices, and users pay for it as part of the price of their new machine; this makes the distinction between hardware and software difficult to capture in import and export figures. This problem is compounded by the fact that, in the current trade nomenclature, there is no distinction between virgin disks and disks containing data, information or programs, so that even software that is sold separately from new computers is not adequately recorded in international trade figures.

The share of developing countries in EDP hardware was quite high, accounting for 40 per cent of exports in 2000. Developed countries - and in particular the United States and Japan - are the main producers of high-end computer products, but Asian countries, particularly Singapore, the Republic of Korea, Malaysia, Thailand and China, are also powerful competitors, especially in the PC sub-segment. Thus, the presence of developing countries is higher in the commoditized IT products, which are characterized by low value- added.

As regards software, the United States is the world's leading exporter, and it has been estimated that 'American off-the-shelf software accounts for 70 per cent of the world market". Among developed countries, Japan, Ireland, Singapore, the United Kingdom, France and the Netherlands are emerging as software industry hubs. Among the developing countries, a number of Asian countries are promoting production of software and software services, in particular India, Pakistan, Malaysia, the Philippines and Thailand among others.

The second largest sub-sector, with 25 per cent of exports, was semiconductors, and it was the one with the largest participation by developing countries, accounting for 43 per cent of exports. Again, the largest producers were the United States and Japan, together with a number of ASEAN countries, whose market share has been increasing steadily. Leading exporters from the ASEAN region are in particular the Republic of Korea, Thailand and Taiwan Province of China.

IT goods is currently low in developed countries and it is quite likely that since developed countries are the main markets for these products, this was one of the factors that enabled the rapid growth of developing countries' exports of IT goods. However, tariffs remain relatively high in the developing world and especially so in least developed countries.

The level of protection is highest in the office equipment and components sub-sectors. The reason for this, with regard to the components sub-sector, is in part that some products included in that sub-sector are difficult to separate from components of an electrical and even mechanical nature. Thus, these products were not subject to the sweeping tariff-cutting exercise that focused on the IT sector.

Even when this is taken into account, the rate applied by some of the least developed countries appears to represent one more obstacle for companies located in those countries in accessing technology at reasonable cost. In order to enable developing countries' manufacturers and service providers to engage in e-business and to take full advantage of the opportunities offered by the new technologies, the tariffs levied on these products need to be reassessed.

In the last three decades a number of countries have used the IT industry as a tool for their development, for a number of reasons. First, the sheer size of the industry now makes it an important investment opportunity. Second, since many segments of the industry do not require a large amount of upfront capital, entry in this sector is relatively easy for countries that have adequate human capital. Third, as mentioned in the previous section, the protection level for the IT industry is relatively low in the major importing markets, and this no doubt was among the factors that favoured the growth of the IT industry in some of the developing countries.

A number of developing countries have therefore undertaken strategies to attract investment in the field of IT and/or develop the IT industry. The IT industry has grown in waves, as regards both technological developments and market demand, so according to one interpretation, the countries that have succeeded in developing an IT local sector were those that recognized and consequently targeted an emerging trend, investing in the production of goods for which the technology was already established, but for which the market was not yet saturated. Some of the South-East Asian countries were, for example, successful in penetrating the PC industry in the early 1980's when PCs relied on a robust technological base and the industry was growing fast.

One clearly emerging new wave in the next few years concerns the development of open-source software. As explained, open-source not only offers promising opportunities to the software industry in developing countries but also is particularly well adapted to fitting in with developing countries' current pattern of hardware production.

Another emerging trend in developing countries is the customization of IT and especially software products for the use of their local or regional markets. In fact, a number of SMEs from developing countries are closely cooperating with transnational corporations in order to make their products or services suitable for the particular needs of a niche clientele or a foreign market.

IT makes to development in its widest possible sense. In fact, IT is among the factors that underpin the globalization taking place in virtually all business sectors. New ICT such as the Internet give companies the opportunity to develop new products, to access world markets at lower costs and to source the goods and services needed in the production process in wider and more competitive markets. This translates into increased efficiency not only at the level of the firm, but also at the level of the business sector and the economy as a whole.

While it is clear that many companies in developing and transition economies are using e-business in a variety of forms, to fully benefit from the new technologies and integrate them into everyday business requires a technological infrastructure and a level of workforce expertise that are beyond the reach of the majority of small and medium sized enterprises in developing countries. It is for this reason that business associations, local and national governments, and international organizations are developing a number of initiatives in order to create a nurturing environment into which the business community can successfully integrate e-business practices.

The present analysis is complementary to these efforts, in that its aim is to offer hindsight on the role of the IT industry in facilitating the adoption of e-business by the local business sector in developing countries. In this connection, the next paragraph presents the survey designed and conducted by the UNCTAD secretariat in order to highlight some of the basic facts of foreign investment in IT in developing countries and especially the relationship between IT transnational corporations and the local workforce and the local business sector.

UNCTAD survey

The UNCTAD secretariat undertook a survey of the determinants of IT companies' investment and use of e-commerce in developing and transition economies. It used several databases in order to identify all the IT companies of a size large enough to justify overseas investment. Information about the sample population, the rate of response and a copy of the questionnaire can be found in annex.

The questions included in the questionnaire were carefully selected and worded in such a way as to minimize the work required of the respondents and to facilitate the analysis of the results. This meant that - with only one exception - multiple-choice questions were preferred to open questions. As an example, many of the questions requested the respondents to choose among alternative strategic options or rank various factors that guide their investment decisions or desired government strategies. Of course, this implied a certain loss of spontaneity and of generality in the answers, which are typical and have to be accepted in these surveys. While a question on the magnitude of worldwide revenue from IT products was included, questions aimed at extracting quantitative information such as the magnitude of planned or existing investment, the revenues from sales at a specific location or the number of personnel working in any given site were deliberately excluded for a number of reasons. First, quantitative information would be difficult for the companies to disclose, and would prevent many from participating in the survey and providing a valuable insight into policies and strategic business options. Second, these questions would not necessarily have given indications about the magnitude of developing country operations. For example depending on the different ownership arrangements and on the business strategy adopted by the mother company or by the local management, a very small upfront investment could result in a larger or a smaller business venture. Including a question on the number of employees could have been equally misleading, depending on what part of the work was subcontracted and on the labour or capital intensity of the goods that were produced.

The answers, which are presented below, are intended to be of assistance in the design of policies and strategies that will not only attract the kind of IT investment that best matches a country's strengths but also allow developing countries and countries in transition to increase the IT competence of the workforce and to deepen the linkages between national firms and IT multinationals. Unless otherwise indicated, the source of all the data presented in the next paragraphs is the UNCTAD survey.

Results of the survey

Composition of the sample

As regards the composition of the sample of respondents, the 35 companies that replied to the questionnaire had a cumulative turnover from IT products of $ 413 billion, which represents around a half of IT worldwide production. The average turnover was $ 12 billion: it should be noted however that this is not the total turnover of the companies - which is even larger - but exclusively the revenue from IT sales.

The sample included companies of different sizes and revealed that even relatively small-scale companies in the field of IT invest in overseas markets. Twelve companies had a turnover of less than $ 1 billion, nine companies between $ 1 and 10 billion, five companies between $ 10 and 20 billion, five between $ 20 and 40 billion, and 3 with more than $ 40 billion.

The survey was not addressed to local IT-producing companies in developing countries for two sets of reason's. First, multinational companies make up an important share of production in the IT sector. For instance, the sum of the revenue of the top ten hardware and of the top ten software producers, according to Fortune magazine, is $ 311 billion, or roughly a third of worldwide IT spending. Secondly, it would have required two different questionnaires to inquire about the local operations of small IT companies and the overseas operations of IT multinationals, so that it was decided that this second line of analysis should be treated separately.

It is interesting to note that the companies which indicated that they invested primarily in hardware and components had an average turnover of $ 18.82 billion, while those that invested primarily in software had an average turnover of $ 4.28 billion. In other words, many of the "smaller" companies in our sample were mainly investing in software. This replicates the underlying structure of the industry: by way of comparison, the 12 largest companies in the field of computer hardware and office equipment had an average turnover of $ 21.3 billion, while the 13 largest software producers had an average turnover of $ 4.3 billion.

Type of ownership arrangements

Respondents were asked to rank the means that their company used in order to establish a presence in developing countries. Companies were given four choices.

The majority of respondents answered that investment was of the greenfield type (building or leasing a facility), while mergers and acquisitions were the least utilized among the available options. Interestingly, this is the reverse of the finding by the World Investment Report: "Over the past decade, most of the growth in international production has been via cross-border M&A rather than greenfield investment". The difference in conclusions may be explained by the fact that the corporate IT sector in developing countries has not yet presented advantageous acquisition targets or merger partners owing to the relative infancy of the entire IT sector.

Our finding could be related to the particular characteristics of the IT industry as opposed to other economic sectors. One should be careful, however, about potential definitional discrepancies. In particular, in our survey, greenfield investment was defined quite loosely to include building or leasing a facility. In other words, this answer could point to strikingly different patterns, such as building a new plant for the production of IT hardware or leasing an office for the distribution of a company's products.

Nevertheless, reading through the answers, and combining this answer with the one on the purpose of investment, led to the conclusion that quite a number of the respondents were indeed undertaking greenfield investment with the intention of starting local production. The prevalence of greenfield investment is a positive sign, because it results in a net increase in the developing countries' production facilities, and can contribute to the overall improvement in macroeconomic and export trade performance. Another important expansion tool, utilized extensively by the respondent companies, was the formation of joint ventures with local companies, whereby the multinational corporation is typically contributing its command of state-of-the-art technology and the local partner the knowledge of the market. In many cases, joint ventures are preferred to the alternative of directly acquiring local companies, because this strategy requires a lower upfront investment, and because continuity in the operations of local companies is preserved.

The relatively low number of companies that chose mergers and acquisitions as their preferred expansion tool could be due to a number of factors, including the fear that local companies may be burdened by debt or tied down by the composition of their workforce.

Utilization of e-commerce by IT multinationals

The respondents declared that - on average - 35 per cent of their purchases and 16 per cent of their sales were done over the net. Reliable statistics on enterprises' use of e-commerce are notoriously difficult to find, and so it was not possible to compare this finding against other figures collected at the worldwide level, as would have been desirable. As a tentative comparison, in the United States, a recent survey by the United States Department of Commerce found that: "E-shipments account for 18.4 per cent of the value of all shipments from US manufacturing plants in 2000". In account of the fact that our sample includes companies from countries that are less advanced in e-commerce than the United States, we can conclude that companies from the IT sector are as would have to be expected - comparatively heavy users of electronic commerce.

In this light, it is interesting to see whether developing countries' operations are able to seamlessly integrate into the multinationals' system of production, which relies on high technology for the execution of contracts with established suppliers.

The respondents were asked what proportion of their developing countries' operations used common information and telecommunication technologies. On a scale of 1 to 10, 10 would represent an answer such as "all developing countries' facilities utilize the technology" and a value of 1 "none of the developing countries' facilities utilize it". A large proportion of developing countries' facilities utilize e-mail and operate a website, but few of them are yet engaging in e-commerce operations such as managing online catalogues, receiving online orders and handling online payments, and more generally becoming integrated into the company's online production system.

It is perhaps for this reason that a rather high percentage of the respondents declared that the various aspects of e-commerce did not facilitate "at all" the setting up and operating of developing countries' facilities (9 per cent). An equal percentage of respondents held an opposite view - namely that e-commerce had greatly facilitated such operations - and the great majority of respondents thought that e-commerce had made things significantly (32 per cent) or somewhat (47 per cent) easier. More research would have to be done to qualify this perception, but it appears that in the operation of overseas facilities the "handshake" and personal contacts still retain their importance in spite of technological advances and that developing countries' facilities continue to be managed utilizing ordinary telecommunications tools rather than the new technologies, in view in particular of the still limited availability of ICT in developing countries.

Location of investment

The respondents were asked to provide details of the regions where they invested or where they intended to invest in the near future, indicating for what purpose they were investing or were intending to invest there. In order to keep the design of the questions simple, the companies were offered six choices: Africa, Eastern Europe, Latin America, Middle East, South-East Asia (ASEAN countries) and other developing countries in Asia (including India and China). The majority of the respondents (70 per cent) indicated that they invested in "other developing countries in Asia", while a slightly lower percentage (67 per cent) in South-East Asia. These regions were followed at a distance by Eastern Europe and the Middle East, and then by Africa and Latin America.

Next, in view of this strong concentration of IT investment, which appears to be even more important than that encountered in many other industries, it becomes interesting to see what are the factors that draw investment to specific countries and what are the consequences of alternative policy actions that countries can take in this regard.

In the first place, the location of the investment was influenced by the location of the mother company's headquarters. On the Asian and Latin American markets, the bulk of the investment was from United States' firms, while in Eastern Europe it was from

East markets the percentages of European and American companies were identical. A surprisingly high percentage of investment in Latin

As for the other factors that directed IT investment to specific markets, the most important was access to markets (market size and potential, proximity to larger markets, participation in regional/bilateral free trade areas), followed by general policy environment (political stability, trade policy, tax policy), cost of production, workforce IT competence, workforce education and investment incentives.

This ranking basically reflects the findings of other surveys - see, for instance, the Foreign Direct Investment Survey 30 - but shows that IT companies attach particular importance to the competences of the workforce. IT multinationals will select the location of their subsidiaries according to fundamental macroeconomic variables, which the country can alter only in the medium to long term. For instance, the most important factor in TNCs decisions appears to be "access to markets": while access is a geographical factor over which the policy maker has little control, partially, it can be enhanced by signing free trade area agreements at the regional level and marketing the country as the potential production hub to service the regional market. The case is similar for factors such as "general policy environment" and "cost of production": Governments can influence them by making the country an enabling environment for investment - both local and foreign- but clearly this can only be a long-term policy goal. Factors such as investment incentives, which can be altered in the short term, are instead likely to have less effect on companies' decisions on the location of investment.

Next, it is interesting to analyze the purpose for which the respondent companies invest in developing regions. The questionnaire gave the companies five choices: Customer Support Service (CSS), Distribution, Production for export on the world markets, Production for local or regional markets, Research and development (R&D) and Other. The most important reason for investment in developing countries was customer support service and distribution, followed by R&D, and production.

Since customer support service and distribution are critical factors that draw IT investment to the different markets, it is safe to assume that IT multinationals will invest more heavily in the very regions in which they are more intensively exporting. Thus, as e-commerce

and e-business lead the business sector in developing countries to make more intensive use of the new technologies more IT investment will flow to those regions. The relative importance of customer support service also points to the growing market which tends to the needs of corporate clients for the customization of hardware and software and which - as was discussed - also offers business opportunities for developing countries.

A cross-analysis of the reasons why multinationals invest in the different regions, accord-To summarize, the findings from the questionnaire point to an intensive concentration of IT investment in South and South-East

Asia and in particular to the concentration of investment for productive and research purposes in those regions. Furthermore, it appears that government policies can only alter investment decisions on location in the medium to long term.

We turn now to the last set of questions, which focused on what actions Governments could take in order to maximize the positive fallback of IT investment, in terms of use of local labour by TNCs and enhancement of workforce skills and in terms of deepening the linkages between TNCs and the local industry.

Labour

A key benefit of FDI - and especially so in the field of IT - is the potential for human resources development. TNCs may in fact act as a powerful pull factor, because they often offer better wages than domestic firms, but at the same time require a higher level of competence. As a result, they stimulate the development of a technically skilled workforce and encourage Governments and households to invest in education. In addition, the characteristics of jobs in TNCs are such that they often require on-the-job training so there TNC investment may have a direct impact on the qualifications of the workforce.

This brings us directly to the next question - how much of the employment generated by the multinationals is local. The respondent companies reported that - on average - local labour represented 79.7 per cent of the total workforce in their facilities in developing countries.

The variation among companies was quite high for this answer, and over half of the companies in the sample reported percentages of 90 per cent and higher. It is also interesting to observe that the multinationals mostly employ skilled 31 labour in their developing countries' facilities: in fact, it represented close to 69 per cent of the total workforceing to the purpose of investment.

It appears quite clearly that investment in production facilities and in research and development - which is the one that most facilitates the transfer of technology from multinationals to local companies - is still heavily concentrated in South and South-East Asia. In fact, while R&D represents 20 per cent of all investment in those two regions, the percentage is only 6 per cent in the Middle East and 7 per cent in Africa. Similarly, investment in production facilities represents 37 per cent of total investment in South-East Asia and only 23 per cent of total investment in Africa.

The respondents were then asked to specify which policy actions would be desirable in order to increase the number of high-skilled local personnel and improve their competencies. The companies were of the view that the most important policy action in this regard was developing and expanding local universities, followed by increasing the quality and reach of primary education.

Subcontractors

One last important dimension that deserves to be explored is that of the linkages between multinationals and local industry. The concept of "linkages" was the central theme in UNCTAD's World Investment Report. 2001, which summarizes its benefits as follows:

> "A key factor determining the benefits host countries can derive from FDI are the linkages that foreign affiliates strike with domestically owned firms. Backward linkages from foreign affiliates to domestic firms are important channels through which intangible and tangible assets can be passed on ... They can contribute to the upgrading of domestic enterprises, provide opportunities for production and employment by domestic suppliers and embed foreign firms more firmly in the host economies".

For these reasons, our survey included a question on the linkages that TNCs made with local firms. The companies that responded to our survey maintain intense linkages with local companies in the host countries. In particular, 65 per cent of companies indicated that they were buying generic office supplies from local firms and 56 per cent that they sourced from them direct inputs into the production process. Only 9 per cent of the firms declared that they did not rely on local partners. Additionally, the respondents were asked to specify which policy actions would encourage them to make further use of local firms. The most important ones are the strengthening of enforcement of contracts either by reinforcing local courts or through international investment agreements, developing the competencies of local firms in the field of IT, improving telecommunication infrastructure and improving information on the stability and financial security of local firms.

4

M-Commerce Opportunities

The most common definition of 'm-commerce' is the buying and selling of goods and services using wireless handheld devices such as mobile telephones or personal data assistants (PDAs). A broader definition that extends m-commerce to "mobile business" may be more appropriate. This involves business-related communication among individuals and companies where financial transactions do not necessarily occur. In the last four years, the growth in the number of mobile telephone users worldwide has exceeded the growth in the number of fixed lines, expanding from 50 million to almost one billion in 2002.

Today, over 90 per cent of countries have a mobile network, and nearly one in every six of the world's inhabitants has a mobile telephone. Almost 100 countries have more mobile than fixed-line telephone subscribers and this will become a global phenomenon in the early part of 2002. The introduction of wireless communications has not only expanded telephony in many developing countries, but also introduced wireless data services which are essential for conducting m-commerce. For many people in developing countries, mobile handsets may be the first and main access route to information and communication technologies (ICT), the Internet and e-commerce technologies.

The challenge is to provide access to the global telecommunications system for a significant number of citizens in developing countries. Mobile communications may be the technology that overcomes the barriers constituted by the high cost of installing fixed-line infrastructure that developing countries continue to encounter.

Current m-commerce applications and trends, including banking and insurance, logistics, securities, and information services, are also reviewed. In addition, regulatory issues related to data security and privacy are assessed. Finally, the main findings and recommendations for developing country m-commerce readiness are presented.

Features of M-commerce

Wireless communications provide the long sought after platform that can make digital data transfer possible in many developing countries. This is due in part to the lower costs of mobile systems relative to fixed networks, the provision of short message services (SMS) and the enabling of wireless Internet connections. In developing countries most mobile services are prepaid using stored value cards. This mitigates post-paid subscription problems of creditworthiness and billing. By mid-2002 there were 300 million mobile telephone users in the Asia-Pacific region.

China has the largest number of mobile telephone users in the world: more than 170 million in mid-2002, with over 400 million forecast by 2005—2006. Europe is an important mobile market with over 300 million subscribers forecast for 2002. The number of wireless communication has already exceeded the number of fixed-line subscribers, and it is expected that in many countries, particularly developing countries, telecommunications operators will continue to rapidly increase the number of mobile subscribers thanks to low infrastructure and operating costs. Surveys in the United States indicate that wireless services are expected to be a major vehicle for customer relationship management (CRM) and that the amount of business management and marketing activities carried out using remote communications is continuously growing.

M-commerce represents the extension of e-commerce merce - B2B, B2C, B2G and P2P-remain. In developing countries mobile business applications, especially when used by small and medium-sized enterprises in remote areas, may become a key method for reaching potential customers, and are expected to be highly important features of m-commerce.

In 2002 worldwide m-commerce revenues are forecast to be just below $50 billion. The United States and Western Europe will dominate actual and forecast revenues through 2005. But by 2005 sales generated in the Asia-Pacific region and the rest of the world are expected to register a significant increase, approaching 40 per cent of the global $225 billion m-commerce revenues forecast. Given that global revenues in 2001 were about $20 billion and very small in regions outside North America and Europe, it is difficult to determine what the major m-commerce transactions have been.

Most m-commerce is B2C where micro-purchases are involved. Larger transactions continue to be conducted using the usual e-commerce methods. The surge in mobile handset use throughout the world, the dramatic growth of the Internet, and the proliferation of PDA (personal data assistants) are expanding the e-commerce market in which m-commerce is expected to flourish. A number of unique advantages of m-commerce have been identified:

— *Immediacy:* Consumers are constantly moving, working, commuting, travelling, socializing and shopping. M-commerce lets them buy goods and services as soon as the need arises.

— *Connectivity*: Users sharing a common location or interest can be instantly connected via text messaging and mobile chat capabilities. Advertisers can use such access to promote products and make special offers with the expectation that subscribers will answer and listen to their messages.

— *Localization*: With the deployment of positioning technologies, such as the global positioning system (GPS), companies can know users' where-abouts and will be able to offer goods and services specific to their location.

— *Data portability*: Users can store profiles of products, company addresses, information about restaurants and hotels, banking details, payment and credit card details, and security information, and access these when needed for purchases or for making contact, all from their mobile handsets.

Internet use has been dependent on personal computers (PCs) and a fixed-line network. And the growth of the

Internet drives e-commerce. Consequently, until the advent of mobile telephone, e-commerce has been dependent on expensive infrastructure and equipment. Today, however, there is a growing convergence of the Internet and mobile communication. Handsets are acquiring functionalities that were limited to desktop PCs only a few years ago.

Many are already running slimmed-down versions of PC operating systems and applications, and the difference between future handheld and desktop devices is likely to be related to the ergonomics of the physical user interface that will be designed to serve a particular purpose, rather than lack of processing power, memory or network accessibility. The ITU reports that 225 countries and territories have dial-up Internet connections - that is, a link to the Internet through a local telephone line.

In 2001 there were over 500 million Internet users, representing 8.2 per cent of the world's population. Global distribution of Internet access, however, remains dominated by developed countries, where over half of the adult population is online. Wireless access is likely to be the principal means of bringing more people in developing countries to the Internet. For that purpose, mobile networks and handsets need to be upgraded to carry data and messaging, as well as traditional voice services. The introduction of "third generation" (3G) and Internet-enabled handsets in North America and Europe is imminent. For the rest of the world, second generation (2G and 2.5G) mobile capabilities have opened-up opportunities for narrow-band Internet access and SMS.

The goal of 3G is to enable broadband mobile Internet and data services capability. After expensive 3G licences were auctioned, mostly in Europe, telecommunication companies accumulated large debts and as a result, mobile broadband infrastructure and 3G have yet to be introduced.

Many telecom operators are questioning whether customers will take-up 3G as rapidly as originally expected. The launch of 3G services has not been as successful as first forecast because potential early adopters are reasonably satisfied with pre-3G service offerings, thereby reducing the attractiveness of 3G's additional features. The situation is quite different for most developing countries.

The first objective of governments and telecommunications authorities is to expand the number of subscribers for mobile telephone voice and short message services. Upgrading to 2.5G or 3G is unlikely in the near future. The burning question for companies that have grown dependent on the Internet as a business vehicle is whether mobile telephony will result more in B2C applications than in B2B applications.

It is impossible on the basis of existing experience to extrapolate what will happen in the years ahead. As regards B2B, there is little evidence that companies will change their purchasing practices because of m-commerce. The short-term potential for e-commerce growth resides with the one billion mobile telephone users, who could supplement existing B2C e-commerce with m-commerce. There is rapid growth in micropayments for small items and information services. The key to increasing traditional B2C purchases such as banking transactions and to trading in securities through m-commerce is the implementation of payment systems that are low-cost and customer-friendly.

Mobile telephony is also helping to eliminate the seemingly endless waiting for a fixed-line subscription. With a mobile network, consumers can simply buy a handset together with a pre-paid card and start using it as soon as the first base stations are in place. As mobile networks are often set up by private sector companies, the investment burden can shift away from the State. The extent of developing countries' involvement in m-commerce is dependent on the access and connectivity of the population to wireless communications. Providing millions of citizens in developing countries with access to wireless voice communications coupled with text messaging, and with an eventual upgrade to the Internet, is crucial to building m-commerce markets in those countries.

Engaging in m-commerce, however, requires more than mobile empowerment. Initiating purchases and completing payments remains a bottleneck for m-commerce in many if not most developing countries. Unless selection, ordering, payment and delivery can be managed at costs that are lower than in traditional commerce, both e- and m-commerce may face serious problems. This may no longer be the case when m-commerce is fully utilized. Because PCs are not required, and fixed-line subscriber fees do not have to be paid, the cost of m-commerce can be relatively low.

A handset may cost less than $100 and prepaid cards have become dominant. An important mobile application that can be used for commercial activities is SMS, particularly because it can exploit the existing wireless infrastructure in many developing countries. However, if there is to be true m-commerce, mobile phones must be Internet-enabled.

Mobile telephony has been taken up to a considerable extent in Asia. There are currently more than 200 million handsets in use, of which more than 120 million are enabled to use data services. In Asia there is much more involvement in m-commerce. The most developed countries in the region - Japan and the Republic of Korea - have large mobile telephone populations with millions of Internet-enabled terminals. The leading developing country example of m-commerce deployment in the region is China. This is not only because the country now has 170 million mobile telephone subscribers, but also because SMS has become very popular and has created a vast potential for m-commerce applications.

Africa has more than 20 million mobile telephone users. By the end of 2001, 28 African nations had more mobile than fixed subscribers. The number of mobile subscribers in 30 sub-Saharan Africa countries, not including South Africa, rose from zero in 1996 to 1.7 million in late 2001. Because most new African mobile subscribers have no fixed line available and very few own or can access a PC, their handset becomes their only communication device. Consequently, there is likely to be a great interest in using mobile handsets for as many applications as possible.

In the least developed countries (LDCs), mobile technology is increasing telephone access in a surprisingly short space of time. Uganda is an example of how mobile telephony has radically transformed access to communications in an LDC over a short period. As a result of the liberalization of the telecommunication sector and the low cost of installing wireless networks, the number of subscribers rose eight times from 1995 to 2000. Uganda's mobile density ranking among LDCs rose from 28th in 1997 to 8th in 2001 and today it has the third largest mobile network in the LDCs.

In many countries, this transition took a little over a year: more mobile telephone users were added to the national network during that period than during the entire period of fixed-line operations. Another example is Afghanistan, where it is expected to take years to fully replace the infrastructures of electricity and fixed-line communications that have been destroyed.

However, this is not the case with wireless communications: inhabitants of Kabul have obtained handsets and began using mobile services with pre-paid cards in April 2002. By the end of May there were more than 2,000 handsets in use, a significant addition to the existing and inadequate 12,000 fixed lines.

Mobile telephone customers in many developed countries are starting to use handsets to make purchases from retail stores, conduct personal banking and make travel reservations, as well as to view sports and news programmes, and search the Web.

In Germany, for example, mobile users are said to "have a moderate attitude toward many new services", yet about 25 per cent are particularly interested in m-commerce possibilities. In the United States mobile phones are often kept in family cars and used as auxiliary communication devices, rather than being carried and used continually by family members.

In Europe, the greatest interest in m-commerce seems to be in Italy whose large population of mobile telephone customers have indicated an interest in paying bills and conducting banking transactions via wireless devices. Mobile service providers allow both prepaid and post-paid account subscribers to register and link their cash/debit cards with mobile phone subscription accounts.

This allows subscribers to conduct mobile transactions for services and goods offered through their particular mobile service provider, for example topping up of prepaid accounts and purchase of theatre tickets. Certain commercial activities using SMS, such as hotel and restaurant reservations, could eventually lead to a growth in m-com-merce applications. The following discussion takes a more detailed look at several promising applications.

Since 1992 SMS has allowed people to send and receive text messages using their mobile phones. Each message can contain up to 160 alphanumeric characters. SMS is the backbone of m-commerce, with the number of messages totalling billions in 2001. One of the greatest concentrations of SMS users is in Singapore, where 52 per cent of phone users utilize SMS more than once a day. SMS use in Australia, China and the Philippines is reported to be almost as high. The global average, however, is 23 per cent.

In December 2000, Filipinos were sending almost 50 million short messages a day, or around 9 per subscriber. The Philippines is the leader in per capita SMS usage, accounting for some 10 per cent of all short messages sent around the world. The Philippines had 8.5 million mobile telephone subscribers in June 2001.

The number of mobile telephones in use exceeded the number of fixed lines in 2000; it continues to grow rapidly and is expected to reach 15 to 20 million. SMS is said to offer a practical alternative for those who do not have a computer; mobile telephone subscribers outnumber PCs in the Philipinnes by 4 to 1. A mobile short message is actually much cheaper than a telephone call. SMS was initially free. A nominal 2 cents charge was introduced in 1999.

In Hong Kong, China, wireless data traffic was underdeveloped because local mobile telecommunications operators were not eager to expand this business while revenue from voice traffic alone was growing rapidly. In December 2001, six local mobile operators announced an agreement to make their SMS interoperable and forecast significant new revenue from SMS in the years ahead.

M-commerce offers vast opportunities to make micro-purchases easier. These can be as simple as buying from a vending machine, paying a parking meter or purchasing gasoline. Among the most widespread m-commerce applications using SMS, is making payments through post-paid accounts linked to debit cards. In the case of subscriptions to information services, the mobile service provider charges the customer through monthly bills. However, in many developing countries a shortage of consumer credit systems and the lack of automated payment systems that can be conveniently used for wireless electronic payments are hampering advancement of m-commerce.

Micro-payments and settlements via wireless are growing rapidly in a number of developed countries. Estimates for 2002 are typically around $1.5 billion. Forecasts for wireless micro-payments speak of $ 200 billion worldwide by 2005, with more than $ 40 billion in the United States.

In the Republic of Korea, mobile Internet customers prefer to integrate charges for purchases into their monthly telephone bills. Japanese often prefer to pay mobile Internet charges and usage fees in cash at convenience stores. Prepaid value cards are widely used in Japan. However, a growing number of services, such as specialized information services, can be charged to monthly telephone bills. A new system will be introduced before the end of 2002 that uses mobile handsets with an infrared interface that would automatically debit pre-paid cards.

The cost of equipping handsets with an infrared interface will be absorbed by savings resulting from operators and vendors not installing new vending equipment. In Japan there is great interest in this new mobile technique. Saving time, simplicity and speed of payments are the main advantages of mobile settlements. The following characteristics are listed in order of importance:

— Payments;

— Rapid payment;

— Record of payment provided;

— Less cash to carry around;

— Point-of-sale convenience;

— Signature not required.

A number of concerns still exist and demonstrate the novelty of mobile settlements and people's lack of awareness about how to take advantage of them. The main concerns are:

— Difficulty in making a payment or a financial transaction;

— Risk to the confidentiality of personal data;

— Difficulties in processing payments, including loss of payments;

Mobile banking is still hampered by the requirement for standardized payment cards and online systems. There has been more success with securities trading, however, where investors can buy and sell shares using their mobile handsets. Other areas are opening up -for example, insurance, where potential customers can receive offers and submit personal details for premium quotes by insurers, all with their mobile phones. Mobile communications provides insurers with yet another way to interact with, and obtain information from, potential customers.

The most immediate benefits are reducing administrative costs and bringing innovative and less expensive services to a wider market. An important facet of mobile technology will be to enable insurance agents and field representatives to provide better customer service. Buying habits are changing in that many customers want online access to product information and quotations and want to pay premiums, compare prices, access and update their policy information and claims status and receive customer service - all online. Regarding direct insurance sales, a vast market of potential buyers could be reached through the use of mobile-based insurance marketing methods. The present level of mobile media richness and the interface quality of commercial handsets may not satisfy regulatory requirements for selling insurance products, including policy delivery and payment, in most countries. Owing to government supervision and policy complexity, mobile insurance may have to wait for 3G before making real m-commerce headway.

Mobile services include all those products provided by securities brokerage firms. Wireless technology enables customers to bypass ordering in person or by telephone, thus opening the securities market to a large number of potential buyers. In addition, brokerages supply financial information and market data to investors through their mobile handsets. This provides individual clients who have online accounts with instant access to the buying and selling of securities. However, because of poor user interface of mobile telephones and PDAs, significant mobile trading is not expected before 2005 and the full roll-out of 3G and associated handsets.

The potential of mobile communications for generating greater efficiency in transport and logistics is widely acknowledged. The movement of goods within developing countries, as well as with regard to imports/ exports, has traditionally been slow and inefficient owing to a lack of modern logistics systems.

ICTs have become the key to achieving efficient logistics. Logistics costs in developed countries add about 12 per cent to the retail cost of a product, whereas in developing countries this may be as high as 20 per cent. Transport and logistics will clearly benefit from the introduction of wireless services and, in doing so, expand m-commerce. Wireless data access will make it possible to follow goods movements throughout the supply and value chain. With the growing use of information technologies in cargo booking, tracking, clearance and delivery by major shipping lines, as well as in customs clearance, ports, warehouses and stock points, external and internal trade will become more efficient. The challenge lies in the introduction of hardware, software and networking which are costly and require technical expertise to operate. Trackability and traceability need to be ensured through interfacing technologies such as ID chips and bar codes. Mobile communications devices will then help link-up the supply chain.

Transport is typically multimodal, ranging from rail-water-air-shipping to express delivery services. The introduction of intelligent transport services further increases the value of mobile communications in the logistics supply chain, in particular for support services such as pick-up and delivery of goods.

News, weather reports, and traffic and map information have increasingly become the services most sought after by mobile telephone subscribers. Since the launch of mobile services in Japan in 2000, as many as 30 per cent of all mobile customers indicate that they are users of those information services. This is three times the PC-based usage of paid information services. There is a charge by mobile service providers of about $2.50 (300 yen) per month for unlimited access to a menu of information services.

Value added text messaging is the use of SMS to provide a content service or product to the consumer at a premium price. The value added to the text message by the application or the content contained therein is assumed to be above and beyond that of a standard text message and the consumer knowingly consents to be billed for that added value. In Ireland, this is known as premium text messaging. It will involve the allocation of a 5-digit short code so that consumers will understand they are accessing premium services and will be prepared to pay for them.

An early entrant will be m-Perium, which will launch an m-payments solution using text messaging that will enable websites to charge their audience for time-metered access on their mobile telephones. Other services that could be available are: event-driven content - sports alerts for a favourite team, personal investment information and alerts, industry sector news alerts, travel information such as localized real-time traffic news, and other local information.

Customer relationship management (CRM) services usually consist of a set of methodologies, software and Internet capabilities that are coordinated and co-integrated and whose purpose is to help an enterprise manage its relationships with customers. Company activities can be very varied and may not always be managed in a coordinated way from a customer-centric point of view. The advantages for consumers of having better coordination between, say, research and development, manufacturing and after-sales services may translate for the company into marketable value-added or increased competitiveness.

Much of any commercial organization's activities, including business operations and customer servicing, falls within the scope of CRM. Therefore, its large size, is not unexpected. CRM can transform knowledge and data stored in companies by applying them, in real time, to existing and potential sales and service opportunities, in particular through access to an enterprise's data, message systems, remote sales force automation and order tracking. It has been forecast that in the United States between 35 per cent and 40 per cent of company sales and support personnel will be using mobile devices within the next two to three years.

Mobile technology is starting to emerge as the newest value-added feature for CRM. Extending CRM to wireless devices will enable enterprises to be more proactive in their marketing and sales by providing continuously updated information to field representatives, as well as by offering customers a broader array of contact and self-service options. Three levels of benefits are expected:

— Wireless CRM enables greater mobilization of the sales force, replacing periodic data synchronization with real-time information concerning products, client status, purchase history, inventory levels, product vendor information, order tracking and related data. The sales force will also have wireless financial transaction capabilities, shortening the sales cycle and increasing enterprise responsiveness.

— Wireless CRM facilitates a higher level of customer support by providing additional contact channels for clients seeking information or technical assistance. By extending customer data to mobile devices, the enterprise enables its support staff to better anticipate and respond to customer issues and enables customers to take advantage of self-service support and transactions via their mobile phones or PDAs.

— Location-based marketing will be an extension of current marketing automation and customer analysis systems. These emerging applications are expected to stimulate m-commerce by extrapolating location-specific buying behaviour to provide information to mobile device users.

M-commerce opens up a myriad of options for new electronic services. These include making appointments, voting, applications for membership or membership renewal and entitlement cards, and alarm systems. Norway provides an excellent example of this diversity of m-commerce.

A survey of frequently purchased items in the Republic of Korea found buying habits similar to those in Japan. About 12 per cent of mobile subscribers indicated that their main preferences are buying movie tickets, cosmetics, banking, audiovisual and electronics products.

The need to protect personally identifiable data has received the attention of national policy-makers and international organizations for more than 30 years. With the advances in wireless communications, concerns have again arisen about loss of control over personal information.

Some 40 countries have adopted national data protection laws, ranging from Canada and Argentina to Sweden and Greece, and Thailand and the Republic of Korea. Internationally, the Organisation for Economic Cooperation and Development and the Council of Europe, have adopted legal instruments for their member countries governing the collection and use of personal data.

Because mobile communications services are new and operators are being licensed to compete with incumbent carriers, a number of policy and regulatory issues must be resolved. Interconnection between fixed-line operators and competing mobile operators has been the major difficulty constraining mobile development.

The predominant conflicts over mobile interconnection have occurred in developed countries where several operators are seeking to gain market share. Developing countries have experienced fewer problems when national regulators have insisted on rapid deployment and fairly priced interconnection rates. Many developing countries, however, have limited geographical coverage for mobile telephone use, some operators charge both caller and receiver, and transmission standards still need to be harmonized.

A new European Community Directive that "adapts and updates existing provisions to new and foreseeable developments in electronic communications and technologies" is now replacing the existing telecommunication Directive. It is expected to be adopted before the end of 2002. The revised Directive stipulates that the location data, giving the geographical position of mobile users' terminal equipment, as in road transport services that provide traffic information and guidance for drivers, may not be used for surveillance purposes. Traffic data in general may be collected and used only with the consent of the subscriber.

It has been recognized that commercial users of wireless communications should be subject to codes of fair personal information practice, established by public law or self-regulation. The Wireless Advertising Association (WAA), an international trade group, has adopted a privacy policy that should be readily available to consumers. Under this policy WAA members should give users notice and choice regarding the use of personal information obtained. It may be used only for the purpose for which it was collected unless users explicitly consent to its being used for other purposes. Furthermore, WAA members are required to make every effort to ensure the security of personal information and, where reasonable, allow wireless subscribers to correct or delete such information.

The specific provisions of the WAA privacy policy require that a member company must make known to potential recipients:

(a) what information is being collected;

(b) its policy on data storage;

(c) the choices available to an individual regarding policy on collection of personal information;

(d) the use of personal information;

(e) any third-party collection of personal information, together with a statement of the organization's commitment to data security; and

(f) what steps the organization takes to ensure data security and access by the consumer to his/her records.

Concerns about e-commerce security are only heightened in the m-commerce domain. Fixed-line Internet and PC-based browser technology provides a media richness and interactivity that can be used to implement technological security and assure commercial partners that transactions are under way safely and surely. In contrast, the present-day mobile interface, be it SMS or WAP, is fairly poor and does not inspire confidence.

Furthermore, worries about data interception in the wireless medium are heightened, unlike in the case of fixed-line access, through an imperfect understanding of the technology. Finally, mobile handsets are more prone to theft and consequential misuse, particularly since they may contain passwords, keys and personal identification numbers (PINs) used to provide the authentication and data integrity required for verifying financial transactions. Security is vital if m-commerce is to become an electronic wallet for micropayments for customers worldwide.

In addition to digital signature laws and regulations, certification authorities are being created by governments, financial institutions and other bodies, or are licensed to private entities, so that parties to e-commerce transactions can know the identity of all entities or individuals involved.

To ensure m-commerce payment interoperability among devices and networks, the financial-services-backed Mobile Payment Forum was established in November 2001. Initial members were Master Card International, Visa International, American Express and the Japan Card Bureau.

The Forum now has 89 members. It is cooperating with the PayCircle consortium and the Mobile Electronic Transactions initiative, supported by wireless and Internet infrastructure vendors and handset manufacturers. The Forum's work should lead to secure m-commerce by migrating existing security mechanisms to the mobile environment, or by installing similar security levels for authentication, data integrity, privacy and non-repudiation. Its work covers both existing and emerging technologies, including symmetric keys and biometrics.

Another organization, Radicchio, is a global initiative of over 50 companies in m-commerce and security industries that promotes m-commerce solutions based on public key infrastructure technology for personal handheld devices and wireless network. This initiative is a cross-industry non-profit organization, representing the interests of mobile operators, system integrators, hardware manufacturers, certification service providers and financial service providers, as well as software houses.

The growth of wireless communications in less than five years has created new voice and data communications services that are essential for launching widespread business and consumer m-commerce applications. It is becoming clear that m-commerce will not parallel earlier expansion of e-commerce. B2C transactions will be far more extensive than B2B transactions. This may be in part the result of already well-established fixed-line channels of e-commerce activities among companies.

Individuals are finding it increasingly attractive to initiate B2C contacts with companies to order purchase products and services. The conduct of m-commerce is limited by difficulties in making electronic payments and concerns about security and privacy of transactions. Technology also plays an important role because mobile terminals must be Internet-enabled in order to provide full m-commerce possibilities.

There is a new dimension of m-commerce that involves introducing products and services that may not directly result in immediate transactions. In the United States, companies use mobile telephony to contact employees, conduct sales and marketing programmes and provide customer care. Enterprises in developing countries may find mobile communications very attractive for marketing in remote locations. Methods to maximize benefits from mobile business clearly require further examination.

Fundamental to a rapid expansion of m-commerce is improved access to mobile services by consumers in developing countries, for which a number of government actions are required. These involve liberalizing the telecommunications market, licensing new mobile operators, creating an independent regulatory body that will establish a fair and competitive market supporting compatible standards and facilitating the interconnection among operators. National Governments should exercise leadership in the adoption of authentication, security and data privacy policies and regulations. Improving connections to the Internet backbone remains vital.

5

E-Publishing: Challenges in the New Millennium

Electronic publishing (e-publishing) is the publishing of information in electronic format. It is implemented by creating, maintaining, archiving and distributing documents using computers and networks. Electronically published materials may be created initially only for electronic transfer, or they may have been converted from material originally published on paper. E-publishing represents an improvement over print publishing technology and is considered a major development that may revolutionize information-related activities in society.

Consequences of e-publishing can be compared to those resulting from Gutenberg's invention of the printing press. This invention is considered the origin of mass communication. For the first time, it became possible to disseminate information and knowledge to large numbers of people who could share it simultaneously. Before then, there were only handwritten books made by monks, scholars and scribes and read only by churchmen, government officials and academics. With the introduction of print, intellectual life was no longer restricted to the elite as publications became more widely available to the general population.

E-publishing can bring about major reductions in the cost of producing and distributing publications, thus making it easier for many individuals and enterprises to participate as authors and publishers and for more titles to be published. Because of increased access to publications by readers and the availability of technology that permits more enterprises to enter the industry, e-publishing can foster a higher degree of competition and increased price transparency.

The benefits of e-publishing may be significant for developing countries. These countries lag behind developed countries in access to published material, including educational publications. Furthermore, their imports of published materials are substantially larger than their exports of those materials. By enhancing the capacity of individuals and enterprises to produce and distribute publications, e-publishing provides great potential for promoting the growth of the publishing industry in developing countries and a reduction in this trade imbalance. A discussion of e-publishing may touch on issues such as technology, the costs of production and distribution, pricing models, industry structure, the quality of published materials and intellectual property.

With the advent of new technologies, the relationships between publishers, the media and consumers which were traditionally based on contractual licensing agreements with copyright protection, have completely changed in ways that make the situation difficult to control. There are many types of publications, including magazines, nonscholarly periodicals, newsletters, pamphlets, booklets, research reports, bulletin boards, catalogues, dictionaries, and encyclopedias. Also, each category may include many subcategories; for example, magazines include general-purpose and specialized ones. Furthermore, even the main categories overlap a great deal in content and format. In some cases, old journal articles by one or more authors are assembled into a book. There is therefore some degree of competition and interchangeability between different types of publications.

Despite this diversity, however, the issues raised in connection with the three selected types of publications are relevant to the other forms as well. The choice is partly based on the fact that newspapers and books have mass markets of a much larger scale than other individual publications. Scholarly journals differ in many ways from the other two types, and also their recent history highlights to a greater degree the economic aspects of publishing, such as cost, pricing models and industry structure.

In each of the selected cases, a general description of the publication is provided in order to give the context in which issues are examined. Also, while the main focus is on economic aspects of e-publishing, brief accounts of technical and other related issues are given in so far as they have economic implications. For example, while the formats in which publications are presented electronically and their functionality are technical matters, at the same time they determine the software and other requirements imposed on users, as well as the searchlights and quality of the published materials, and these are important economic dimensions.

Newspapers

Newspaper are serials usually issued daily or weekly. Their primary function is to report public news of general interest, although they may also include features, commentary and advertisements. Newspaper publishing enterprises range in size from small, locally based publishers to national and international ones owned by international conglomerates or industrial groups. All countries around the world publish newspapers, but the number of newspapers and the circulation of individual newspapers vary widely.

There is presently a great deal of interest in on-line newspapers, and numerous newspapers are now posted on the Internet. Some directories of online newspapers list over 10,000 newspapers covering practically every country around the world, including least developed countries (LDCs). While there is no evidence that all the listed online newspapers are fully functional, the sheer numbers involved demonstrate the overwhelming perception by newspaper publishers of the importance of an online presence and also the existence of demand for electronic newspapers.

The volume and quality of content and the level of sophistication of the browsing functionality vary considerably between newspapers. Most online newspaper publishers maintain print versions alongside the digital versions. The majority of the latter can be accessed through the World Wide Web (WWW) and use the hypertext mark-up language (HTML) format, making them readable with a standard Internet browser. This means that the reader has to be connected to the Internet in order to read the newspaper. An alternative means of distribution for e-newspapers is e-mail. For e-mail distribution, besides HTML, formats such as PDF (portable document format) and plain ASCII text are also used. E-mail distribution avoids the necessity of establishing an Internet connection at the time of reading the newspaper. Further, the PDF format may allow the publisher greater control of layout and content so that material cannot be quickly and easily copied, modified, and then distributed by third parties.

Some newspapers have automated search and archiving capabilities that enable readers to access back issues containing previous related articles and other background information for a given news item. In some cases, news items appearing in a current issue of the print version are reported in greater detail or with additional data in the online version. For example, the latter may contain more pictures, longer narratives, full interviews, and so on. In addition to text, online newspapers may offer other features, such as audio, video, graphics and charts, that enhance the news presentation. Links may give access to online libraries through which readers are connected to various reference sources. Another service is the provision of personalized newspapers, whereby a reader can receive an individualized selection of articles published in a given newspaper.

To achieve this, the reader identifies preferred subjects such as current events, sports or cultural and political issues and the newspaper automatically designs a personalized edition containing articles that match the reader's interests. Yet another useful feature of online newspapers is continuous updating of news, something that would be too costly to accomplish for print newspapers. However, in spite of the possible technical and economic viability of a continuous updating, apparently at the moment only a few newspapers are providing continuous updates perhaps because most newspapers are still closely linked to their print counterparts in their production systems.

The majority of online newspapers are free and provide unrestricted access to their ripostes. Some, while free of charge, impose access restrictions by requiring the reader to enter an ID and password, both of which are issued after the reader has provided a selection of personal information. Other papers employ differentiated pricing whereby parts of the paper are free while other parts that contain special information require a subscription.

Some papers even offer two separate online versions, one free and the other subscription-based. Where the entire online version is free, the funding comes from advertisements appearing in the print versions and, in some cases, in the online version as well. Some observers think that online versions are being offered for free merely on an experimental basis to allow publishers to gain information about readers and their Internet habits. In due course, more and more newspapers are expected to charge for access to their websites. While this change is already happening, it has not yet become widespread. In some cases the online version comprises only selected parts of the print newspaper, which obliges readers to obtain the print version if they wish to access all the articles. Unlike print journalism, where interaction with readers is largely limited to letters to the editor, online newspapers permit wide-ranging contacts between and among readers, editors and journalists that allow the newspapers to receive feedback from readers.

E-publishing has had an impact on newspaper journalists trained for or experienced in print publishing by obliging them to learn new methods of information collection and reporting. For example, it requires them to use skills needed for online presentation, including the use of video, animation and audio. Journalists are emerging who can combine information technology skills with elements of traditional news reporting.

Scholarly journals

Scholarly journals play a role as channels and sources of information important to society, in fields including scientific discovery, medicine, public policy, business, technology, industrial development, and so on. Articles in scholarly journals are based on original research and written by experts or scholars in specific academic or professional fields, as opposed to newspaper journalists. A published article is usually identified with the author who derives recognition from it. Journals typically have a review board consisting of peers or other scholars in the field that decide which submitted articles will be accepted for publishing. Unlike newspapers, scholarly journals have limited interest for the general public.

However, they have dedicated markets comprising authors and readers who depend on them as publishing outlets for career advancement and as sources of scholarly or professional knowledge. Therefore, individual journals tend to have a higher degree of continuity and less demand elasticity than, for example, newspapers. Furthermore, the major stakeholders for scholarly journals - journal publishers, scholars, public and private institutions and libraries - are different from those for newspapers, and thus some of the underlying issues in relation to e-publishing are different. On the consumer side, libraries play a pivotal role in the purchasing of scholarly journals, accounting for the bulk of subscription revenue.

Many scholarly journals have traditionally been published by nonprofit academic associations, although there is increased participation by commercial publishers. In recent years, scholarly journals have faced severe financial problems resulting mainly from escalating subscription prices and from budgetary constraints faced by libraries, which are the major subscribers.

Increases in the prices of journals appear to be the result of a combination of factors including rising production costs and the ability of publishers to charge as much as the market can bear. The latter ability is enhanced by the monopoly enjoyed by certain publishers and by the presence of inelastic demand. It has been suggested that the largest journal publishers may be playing the role of price leaders and influencing the prices of the other publishers.

Another possible explanation is that too many journals have entered the market in recent years, which has led to reduced circulation for individual journals and in turn to an increase in the average fixed costs. Interestingly, journals published by commercial publishers differ substantially from the prices of those published by nonprofit professional associations.

Like newspapers and other publications, journals are now embracing electronic publishing. Scholarly or academic electronic journals have shown a very high rate of growth. As of 2000 nearly 20,480 active serials or periodicals were available online. These included academic/scholarly journals, bibliographies, bulletins, consumer journals, directories, government publications, newsletters and newspapers. According to the database, online was the leading single format alternative to print, followed by microform/fiche/film for 13,580 periodicals. Equally significant, Ulrich's reports that as of October 2000 a total of 2,401 online-only serials had been launched, most of which were still active.

E-publishing of scholarly journals is likely to expand readership, especially in developing countries where learning institutions are usually undersupplied with journals for budgetary reasons, and where scholars have limited access to outlets for scholarly publication. It also makes possible the introduction or expansion of advertising, which traditionally has not been a major source of income for scholarly journals.

In many ways, the business models used for electronic journals resemble those for online newspapers. Many journal publishers offer both print and electronic versions of each issue, what is referred to as parallel or dual publishing. At present this model is useful in that it gives users a choice, particularly at a time when e-publishing is still at a formative stage. It seems that many publishers of scholarly journals are unwilling to make a complete shift to electronic only publishing because this new business model is still being tested.

It is too risky to abandon print publishing, which continues to be the mainstay of the publishers' cash flow. Similarly, some subscribers (e.g. libraries) prefer to have access to electronic journals without abandoning the print versions, for which they have well-established cataloguing and archiving systems. In some cases, the electronic versions are full-text versions of the print issues, while in others they present tables of contents only, or selected parts or articles of the print version. Presenting the table of contents alone does not constitute true e-publishing, and probably the real objective is to use the electronic version to advertise the print version.

On the other hand, presenting selected articles is an attempt to provide free access without jeopardizing the volume of subscriptions. In other cases the electronic journal contains additional information, including raw data used for research, thus allowing other researchers to test the same data in different ways.

Some e-journals provide hypertext links, which are particularly useful in scholarly publishing, given the large number of sources that researchers usually consult in a given research project. Interactivity and searching capability are also being extended to the creation of databases, which bring together texts, indexes and abstracts of articles published in different journals.

E-journals employ more or less the same formats for delivering content as those used by newspapers, that is, HTML and PDF. When journals make extensive use of symbols and graphics, these may be inserted into HTML or PDF in their original graphic file formats, of which the GIF and JPEG formats are the most common.

Like newspapers, scholarly journals adopt a variety of pricing and licensing methods. Some publishers bundle the electronic version with the print subscription by providing free access to the electronic version to those who subscribe to the print version, while others charge an additional fee for access to the electronic one. Still others supply the electronic version as the base price, and the price of the print version is added to the electronic one. Yet other publishers use separate pricing for print and electronic versions, as well as charging per article accessed by the reader. In most cases, institutions such as libraries pay a site license fee for electronic access and must then ensure that only entitled persons in the institution get access. The licenses are negotiated separately even in cases where an institution also subscribes to the print version.

The question of the cost of e-publishing is contentious. First-copy costs are high, although the marginal costs of printing additional copies and physical distribution costs are low. On the other hand, the processing of articles, marketing and administrative costs are costly. Some studies have suggested that costs are considerately lower for e-journals than for print journals. For example, a study commissioned by Industry Canada concluded that the production and distribution of a new e-journal could be 28 to 48 percent less expensive than the cost of the print counterpart.

However, some publishers contend that set-up costs for e-journals are high and that the largest share of publishing costs is fixed, including editing and marketing costs, which apply to both print and electronic publishing. Also, the additional capabilities that come with e-journals lead to cost increases. Some publishers enter e-publishing with no experience in the business and are obliged either to invest in developing in-house the skills and competencies required for e-publishing or to contract out the technical work of website development and maintenance and to support outside vendors in acquiring the necessary state-of-the-art technology.

Users of e-journals see an increase in other fixed costs, for example, involving site licenses, new cataloguing systems, the hiring of extra library staff members to manage journal access, the training of staff members and costumers in the use of the new system, and hardware costs including computers and printers. Some costs (e.g. printing) are actually passed on to end users.

Thus, overall, the comparison of costs between e-journals and print journals is inconclusive. This uncertainty clearly presents a dilemma for publishers as well as their main customers. For the publishers, it is not clear which model will prevail in the long run. In the short run, the parallel printing system is proving to be very costly.

As e-publishing expands, some readers move to e-journals, thus reducing the subscription base for print journals without the former fully compensating the latter in the form of increased revenue from e-journals. This tends to oblige publishers to increase subscription rates for print journals, which in turn encourages libraries and other institutions to cut back further on subscriptions.

The financial difficulties faced by scholarly journals that were referred to earlier have led to a number of initiatives with implications for e-publishing. Even though there is no general agreement regarding the relative costs of electronic and print versions of journals, some observers have encouraged self-publishing by scholars and the formation by scholars and libraries of network-based electronic publishing projects as a way of bringing down journal prices.

Self-publishing by scholars is becoming viable as new technology makes it feasible for authors to format their own papers. It is also significant to note that peer review and editing are usually offered for free by other scholars, and thus self-publishing would not involve prohibitive costs for authors. Partly to implement such a strategy, scholarly and professional associations have been urged to use electronic submission of manuscripts and to distribute journals to subscribers electronically. These initiatives may help account for a large increase in the number of e-journals launched by scholars in recent years.

However, the academic community has not fully accepted e-journals as a form of scholarly publishing. E-journals are considered by some to have lower quality and prestige than print ones, and usually authors of articles in e-journals are denied academic credit for these publications. It has been pointed out, for example, that some e-journals cut costs by eliminating professional copy editing and peer review. However, it appears that the lack of recognition of e-journals for academic credit is partly due to inertia and uncertainty vis-à-vis a new system.

Proponents of e-journals have pointed out that even scholarly print journals evolved over time, at a pace dictated largely by developments in scholarly culture rather than by technological developments. They note that scholars tend to be conservative in their intellectual pursuits. What matters most are the norms and standards being enforced rather than the technology used for publishing and delivery. Technically, manuscript submission and peer reviews can be managed through e-mail. Similarly, editing and correction can be performed electronically.

Furthermore, quality can be ensured if publishers and libraries establish codes of best practices for authors regarding such matters as peer review. There is nothing inherent in e-publishing that prevents scholars and publishers from maintaining high publishing standards. Some observers have suggested that electronically managed peer review could be rendered faster, more efficient and more transparent than the traditional process. For example, the use of the Internet could permit contact with a large population of possible peer reviewers and a much faster circulation of manuscripts. It could also allow open peer comments, thus providing a supplementary level of review. Also, available information shows that e-journals do care about quality; for example, a study on e-publishing acceptance rates revealed that rates for accepted and rejected manuscripts were not lower for e-publications than for print publications.

Authors of journal articles are able to circulate the initial drafts of their articles before they are eventually submitted for publishing. Electronic publishing facilitates this process as authors can carry out the distribution more cheaply and to a wider readership online. Authors can use pre-print servers to send manuscripts to central databases or post them on directories that are accessible to the general public. Preprints create opportunities for authors and help alleviate the problem of high journal prices, but at the same time they create difficulties for publishers: readers who can access preprints for free have little or no incentive to subscribe to the journal, and budget-constrained libraries, too, may tend to rely largely on free preprints.

Books

Books are the single most numerous type of publication outside the category of periodical publications. For statistical purposes "book" as a "non-periodical printed publication of at least 49 pages, excluding covers". Eelectronic books (e-books), have aroused great interest in the publishing industry, with some expecting that e-books would completely revolutionize book publishing. Particularly note worthy was the publication by a best-selling commercial author, Stephen King, of "Riding the Bullet" as an online-only book in 2000. The considerable demand for the book convinced the industry, including traditional bricks and-mortar publishers, that there was really a potential for e-books. At the time it was predicted, for example, that sales of digital books (e-books), digital downloads and print-on-demand books would grow from $9 million in 2000 to $414 million in 2004.

E-books are created as computer files that can be read by various mechanisms - computers, personal digital assistants (PDAs) or special hand-held book reading devices using proprietary software. They can be delivered to the reader either as downloads from the Internet or as e-mail file attachments. E-books can also be made available on diskette and CDROM. They use a variety of file formats and can be read using various operating systems or in files that are equipped with reading software. These various formats provide different functionalities, for example, an e-book created as an HTML file gives the capability to include multimedia features with audio, video and animation

Demand for E-books

There is an apparent lack of consensus regarding how well the market for e-books has performed. Some analysts point out that there have been very few commercial success stories between 2000 and 2002. It is pointed out that most established book authors continue to publish with traditional print publishers, and those in the industry who had forecast the rapid growth of e-books no longer support those expectations. On the other hand, some industry actors continue to support and invest in e-book-related activities contending that e-books have enjoyed high growth rates and will continue to do so.

Furthermore, a number of print publishers are preparing to distribute their existing titles electronically. Other interests such as the Open eBook Forum are promoting e-books by raising reader awareness of the benefits of e-books. Indeed, supporters of e-books suggest that the real issue is not that there is a poor market for e-books but that the initial growth forecasts were exaggerated. A quick look at promotional materials indicates that a large number of e-books are being advertised and points to the existence of an impressive array of e-book distributors, publishers as well as on-demand publishers. The problem in making an independent assessment is to determine the actual volume of e-book sales.

Another relatively new distribution format, print on demand (POD), is a sort of combination of e-publishing and print publishing. This technology allows a book to be stored as an electronic copy and be printed and bound only according to the number of copies actually demanded or paid for. For book publishers, printing on demand solves the perennial problem of having to print copies without being certain of the actual number required by the market, and then having to absorb the resulting unrecouped production and storage costs.

Benefits of e-books

Where the print publishing model prevails, many books that are written are never published. Because of the high cost of editing, formatting and printing, the publishers tend to select only the "best" books, largely on the basis of expected sales. As a result, publishers have tended to dominate the process of deciding which books get published and which do not.

E-books allow authors to publish online themselves at an affordable cost. This increase in outlets and opportunities has empowered authors to decide what materials actually get published. Further, as e-publishing increases competition between publishers, e-publishers are more willing to publish books that would have been rejected in print publishing.

Some e-publishers are willing to work more directly and closely with them than traditional publishers would be. Also, some e-book publishers assist authors with the editing and distribution of e-books. The books may be advertised on the publisher's website, and other services may also be offered - for example, copyright and ISBN registration and registration in the Books In Print database as well as with major online book distributors. This generosity may be explained by the fact that many e-publishers are new to the industry and are in the process of establishing business networks.

E-publishing can also provide improved customer service and can allow authors to receive quick feedback from readers about their publications. For example, authors can establish direct contact with readers by providing e-mail addresses and websites through which readers can express their views and suggestions concerning a book. Such information may help authors in preparing updates or new editions of their works. Also, e-publishing has been credited with increasing the royalties paid to authors. It is reported, for example, that on average e-publishers pay authors royalties in the range of 20 to 30 per cent of the net price received from sales of a book, compared to the royalties of 8 to 10 per cent typically paid by print publishers. Some e-publishers provide even higher royalties, such as a 50-50 split of royalties with authors.

As the cost of Internet access declines, e-publishing stands to benefit from an increase in the number of readers to whom publications are distributed without consequential cost increases. The cost of distributing an e-book remains the same regardless of the number of people reading the book, subject to the size of the bandwidth available. Authors who self-publish are able to eliminate intermediaries nd deal directly with readers, thus reducing transaction time and other transaction costs, although they must pay for marketing costs. Thus, overall, e-publishing lowers barriers for new entrants and offers the potential for a much greater number of individuals to publish their books which in turn creates the potential for a large increase in published titles.

Largely due to economies of scale, traditional print publishing requires books to be printed in large numbers in order to maximize opportunities for profitability, although the existing market may not ensure that the whole print run is sold. Printing numerous copies of a book has the disadvantage of tying up capital and also involves considerable costs for shipment, warehousing, inventory and distribution to retailers. The alternative, namely printing fewer copies, poses the risk of running out of stock, which can result lost sales opportunities.

Also, small print runs are less profitable than large ones, as unit printing costs tend to decrease with increasing numbers of printed copies.

The tendency towards large print runs is due largely to the difficulty of ascertaining demand. Available information shows that, while book publishers often distribute large numbers of copies of printed books to retailers, eventually many copies are returned unsold to the publishers.

The above problems can largely be eliminated with e-books. As e-publishing minimizes the amount of printing, the need to determine demand is also minimized. Physical transportation of books is significantly more costly than the distribution of e-books. Similarly, e-publishing reduces or eliminates warehousing and inventory costs.

E-publishing has still other benefits. New editions can be produced more frequently than in print publishing. Publishers can publish shorter titles, reprints and books that are out of print, with few or no overhead costs. E-publishing also makes it possible to sell parts of a book or other publication and thus provide new sales opportunities for a given publication. Length limitations are far less important than in print publication, and authors can include additional content such as annexes, additional data, and so on, which is not always feasible in print versions.

Unlike printed books, which eventually run out of print and tend to remain available in bookstores for relatively short periods of time, e-books can theoretically remain available for any length of time. Generally, e-publications have lower sale prices than their print counterparts. For example, the prices of e-books in a particular category might range from $1 to $6 whereas comparable paperbacks might sell for $6 to $10. Like e-newspapers and e-journals, e-books enable the use of features such as sound, video, automatic cross-referencing and interactivity. They also allow readers, through hyperlinks, to be linked to other texts, audio, video or other digital content outside a book that is accessible on the Internet. Further, they permit publishers to reach global markets more readily.

Disadvantages of e-books

E-books have the disadvantage of being less portable than printed books. An e-book has to be read on a computer screen or using an e-book reader. Generally, text is harder to read on a computer screen than in print form; characters are not as clear, and looking at a screen for extended periods of time can be tiring. As regards e-book readers, consumers have been concerned by their cost and by the fact that all devices are not compatible with all e-book formats. This obliges customers to keep track of which e-books can be read on their systems, and creates difficulties for publishers in deciding on which formats to use.

Cost comparison

The relative costs of online and print publishing are of major concern to publishers because they are a major factor in deciding whether to get involved in e-publishing. At first glance, e-publishing appears to be less expensive than print publishing, since in the former the marginal costs of printing and physical distribution, are low or nonexistent. However, a more meaningful comparison must consider both fixed and variable costs. Fixed costs include the cost of editors and other staff and the technology infrastructure needed for production. Some of these costs may be higher in e-publishing than print publishing. For example, staff costs may rise because of heavy dependence on skilled technology workers.

However, today most book "manuscripts" are prepared as computer files and are delivered to the printer in electronic format. Converting these files to the widely used HTML or PDF format should not require substantial additional resources. Also, increased competition may create greater demand not only for high-level customer services but also for high-quality publications with sophisticated functionality. As in the case of journals, therefore, there appears to be no clear consensus, at least in the current run transition atmosphere, as to whether, overall, e-books are less costly than printed books.

Since e-books are a relatively new form of publishing, publishers are still searching for the most appropriate pricing models. Because of this and other factors, including efforts by institutions such as libraries to overcome budgetary constraints, the pricing of e-publications has generally become fairly complex and in many ways contentious.

E-Publishing in Developing Countries

The preceding section outlined the state of the art in e-publishing and the potential benefits this model offers. As regards the actual growth of e-publishing, it was mentioned that some sectors, such as e-journals, have seen much progress in spite of uncertainty caused in part by the ongoing crisis of high journal prices in the face of limited library budgets. On the other hand, there are clearly opposing perceptions concerning e-books, with some observers feeling that e-books do not yet have a significant presence and are not likely to do so soon, while others think their market role is substantial and growing.

E-publishing is already having a significant impact, given, for example, the number of online newspapers and e-journals currently in existence. There is therefore justification for taking a positive view of this new technology and supporting e-publishing activities for the benefit of all stakeholders in the publishing chain. The slow growth of e-publishing should not be interpreted to mean that this form of publishing has no future. Historically, a number of other technologies, including press printing, have taken decades to have a major impact on society.

E-publishing uses technology and business models that make it easier for individuals and small enterprises to publish cost-effectively. It also allows their publications to reach a global readership at a minimal cost. The net effect is to enable enterprises in developing countries to compete with established publishers, although initially they may need to rely on niche markets at the national or regional level.

Publishers and users in developing countries have lagged behind their developed- country counterparts. This lag can be attributed to a variety of factors, including the low level of Internet connectivity, without which e-publishing is not possible. However, more fundamental problems exist that are directly linked to the publishing industry itself.

Some of the problems concerning publications in developing countries and their implications for the growth of e-publishing are summarized below. The publishing industry as a whole is generally less developed in developing countries than in developed ones.

Developing countries, with a much larger share of the world population, had more or less the same number of newspapers as developed countries. Even more significant, in developed countries the volume of circulation per 1000 inhabitants was more than twice than in developing countries. In this connection, other sources show that in developing countries with a sizable publishing industry the main publishers are branches of major publishing houses in developed countries. Other indicators, such as the number of book trade organizations, show the same uneven distribution across countries.

The following summary by the UNESCO Institute for Statistics provides a succinct picture of the uneven distribution of the production of published materials and access to such materials:

— Over 50 per cent of countries worldwide have an estimated daily newspaper circulation of 50 copies per 1,000 inhabitants.

— In more than half of the world's countries, there are fewer that 10 newspaper titles. Only 8 per cent of countries have over 100 newspapers.

— Around 50 per cent of countries worldwide produce, on average, less than one book per inhabitant per year; 30 per cent produce between one and three books per inhabitant; and 20 per cent produce four or more books per inhabitant annually.

— Around 60 per cent of countries have fewer than 50 copies of school textbooks per 1,000 inhabitants, while just 20 per cent of countries have more than one textbook for every inhabitant.

— Around 70 per cent of countries worldwide provide fewer than 200 public libraries per million inhabitants; 16 per cent provide between 200 and 500 libraries; and 15 per cent provide more than 500.

— In nearly 50 per cent of countries worldwide, all the libraries combined contain less than one book per inhabitant; 20 per cent contain between one and three books per inhabitant and 30 per cent contain four or more books per inhabitant.

The following observations further illustrate the poor state of publishing in developing countries:

— There is limited information on what publications are published in developing countries. For example, only a few articles published in developing countries are listed in the world's major journal indexes and book directories. This lack of information undermines readers' ability to access these publications and authors' ability to research opportunities for publishing in these countries.

— Partly because of the above and for reasons of quality and prestige, many scholars in developing countries tend to publish with publishers in developed countries, thus failing to contribute to the growth of the local publishing industry or those of other developing countries.

— While many scholars from developing countries strive to publish their work in developed countries, a number of factors such as competition for authorship and biased peer review, make it relatively difficult for developing-country authors to be published. In other words, authors in developing countries fail to realize their full publishing potential due to limited access to publishing outlets or lack of knowledge about the outlets.

— High journal costs have been exacerbated by a proliferation of scholarly journals on different subjects. This means that many journals available on the market are not being purchased and therefore, are not used by readers. Journals published in developing countries thus face particularly stiff competition from those of developed countries. The latter have a larger readership base, which generates a more substantial cash flow, ensuring regular publication and consistent quality.

— Some journals and textbooks produced in developing countries have relied on government and corporate sponsorship, but these sources have decreased with the countries' overall poor economic performance in recent years. Also, limited readership has meant limited advertising revenue.

The problems facing publishing in developing countries can be overcome or reduced by e-publishing. As was mentioned earlier, the technology and business models applied in e-publishing may provide business opportunities for enterprises, including small ones, in developing countries. In recognition of the potential social and economic impact of publications, a number of national and international initiatives have been launched to promote e-publishing and access to e-published materials in developing countries.

Such initiatives are new and there is little information regarding their current status and successes or failures. It is notable, however, that the provision of access to e-publications to institutions in developing countries for free or at reduced prices appears to be similar to pricing models that are used by a large number of publishers worldwide. It was pointed out that free access was at times used as a marketing strategy which could change in due course. On the other hand the initiatives involving the access to publications produced by developing country publishers, if successful, could result in genuine growth of e-publishing in the developing countries.

Copyright Issues

Intellectual property is an intangible form of property and includes four types of human works that are protected by copyright laws: inventions (patents); symbols, names and images (trademarks); designs used in commerce (industrial designs); and literary and artistic works (copyright). Copyright law grants the author of a work the exclusive right to reproduce the work, prepare derivative works and perform and display the work publicly. Copyright protects published and unpublished literary, scientific and artistic works in any form of expression. Protection automatically occurs when works are actually created and fixed in a tangible form. Registering copyright may be convenient for commercial or litigation purposes but is generally not necessary to obtain a valid, enforceable copyright.

Since the advent of new technologies in the 1990s, the development of adequate national and international copyright legislation has been of particular concern. Indeed making works accessible via the Internet or other digital channels, authors and publishers are losing control over the distribution of their works. The concern of copyright owners has thus taken on new and challenging dimensions.

New technologies enable anyone to make exact copies of a work and share them almost anonymously with others. The Internet allows people to steal contents freely and share them with others using tools such as peer-to-peer technology (P2P). P2P on the Internet is a network that allows computer users with the same type of networking software to access files from one another's hard drives. This was the technology that was employed by millions of Napster users.

While basic computer equipment is needed for carrying out piracy, copying and distribution process have been dramatically facilitated by advanced digital technology. Cases have been recently reported in which books were being illegally translated or copied, sometimes even before their official release.

This happened, for example, with J.K. Rowling's famous "Harry Potter" series. Before the advent of the Internet and related technologies, many countries were already facing copyright infringement on a large scale. The illegal copying of books presents a real danger to the survival of the legal publishing industry. For example, the UNESCO Courier in its March 2001 edition published figures showing that : while the legal publishing industry annual turnover in Latin America and Spain is $5 billion, the illegal business makes $8 billion.

The copyright issues related to the publishing industry are similar to those faced by the software and music industries, both of whose products are copyright protected. However, piracy of published works, including books, newspapers and journals, has not yet reached the same level in terms of volume, monetary value and popularity as that of music, for example.

Nevertheless, it is likely to become a serious problem as e-publishing takes off. It has been reported that digital piracy (involving software, music, films and books) is responsible for multi-billion-dollar loss annually. So far, thousands of books are said to have been illegally exchanged on the Web in 2001; figures or estimates are not available for journals and newspapers.

Developed countries, as major exporters of intellectual property, have made great efforts to ensure its protection. Since the 1990s, a worldwide trend toward the harmonization of national laws has been influenced by international negotiations that led, in particular, to the adoption of international agreements such as the WTO Agreement on Trade-Related Aspects of Intellectual Property (TRIPS), the 1996 WIPO Copyright Treaty and the WIPO Phonogram Treaty, known as "the WIPO Internet Treaties".

The increasing economic importance of intellectual property rights makes them a more and more prominent issue in trade relations between countries. The main argument advanced in international debate in support of the protection and enforcement of intellectual property rights is that they lead to greater international trade for the benefit of all.

Given that developed countries are the major exporters of intellectual property, the intention is clearly to protect their exports by keeping pirated products out of the destination markets. The main justification of copyright for developed countries has always been economic.

The largest exporter of intellectual property rights is the United States. In 1990, the United States formed the International Intellectual Property Alliance (IIPA), which divided copyright-based industries into four groups, and provided statistics on their contribution to gross domestic product (GDP), employment and trade in the United States. The IIPA 2002 Report confirms the important role of copyright-based industries which represent one of the fastest-growing sectors of the economy, making significant contributions to domestic employment and revenue growth as well as to international trade.The Report states that in both developed and developing countries, studies have generally reported contributions to GDP in the range of 3 to 6 per cent.

According to the Report, it is estimated that in 2001 the core copyright industries in the United States accounted for 5.24 percent of the country's GDP, or $535.1 billion - an increase of over $75 billion from 1999. Over the last 24 years (1977 - 2001), the copyright industries' share of GDP grew more than twice as fast as the remainder of the U.S. economy (7 per cent vs. 3 per cent). The IIPA's estimate of the revenues generated by foreign sales/exports of selected U.S. core copyright industries in 2001 was $88.97 billion, an increase of over $52.78 billion from 1991. To put these figures into perspective, it is necessary to look at the extent the importance of trade losses in the United States due to copyright piracy.

IIPA's estimate of total trade losses for 2001 was $9.4 billion, an increase of $898 million from 2000. Business software applications represented 29.3 per cent of the total trade losses in 2001, closely followed by record and music, losses related to this sector increased from $2.9 billion in 2000 to $3.2 billion in 2001.

Estimates related to book losses, which in 2001, represented 10.3 per cent of the total trade losses at $650.8 million, while their value was $671.8 million in 2000. IIPA's estimates that worldwide loses due to piracy of United States copyrighted materials are in the annual $20-22 billion range, and does not include estimates due to Internet piracy. The United States' trade losses from piracy are increasing and are expected to grow even more with the development and expansion of new technologies.

In most developing countries, copyright issues have not acquired the same urgency because copyright-based industries remain smaller. As was pointed out by the World Bank in 1999, from the viewpoint of developing countries, the relevance of copyright is usually limited to artistic and literary works and the motion picture and television industries. With the expansion of Internet use, it is expected that copyright- based industries will grow in locations offering adequate IT skills and lower production costs, as has happened in some Asian countries in recent years. Efforts made by developing countries to address issues concerning national and international copyright legislation will occur when the capacity of local industries to generate intellectual property increases.

Copyright laws have been technology-driven and have tended to follow the development of technologies pioneered by the developed world. In the publishing industry, the invention of the printing press, computers and new technologies has led to reform of copyright legislation. The Statute of Ann, enacted by the British Parliament in 1710, known as the corner stone of copyright, responded in particular to booksellers' fear of their books being counterfeited and illegally distributed. Further to the Statute of Ann, national legislation was enacted in several countries: in 1790 the United States promulgated its first federal copyright statute, and thereafter several Western European countries (France, Germany, Austria and Spain) enacted laws recognizing authors as the owners of rights in their works.

In some developing countries, the laws regarding the protection of intellectual property were modelled on existing laws of developed countries. As the number of copyright-based industries in developing countries is generally quite low, the development of national laws was not high in the development agenda. Even developing countries that have implemented and ratified national and international agreements still do not fully meet their obligations in enforcing these laws. However, with the growth of copyright-based industries facing competition from foreign products, many developing countries have now realized the impact of copyrights and more generally intellectual property rights on their economies following.

Copyright protection is provided in the Berne Union of the Protection of Literary and Artistic Property, known as the Berne Convention. The Convention establishes standards for protection of copyrights in literacy and artistic works. It envisages the principle of automatic treatment by providing protection to artistic works and national treatment that allows the courts of a country to apply national laws to offences occurring within that country. To date, 140 member countries have ratified the Berne Convention.

More recently, the concern over digital rights has forced national, regional and international authorities to adapt their legislation to face the new threats posed by virtual and global distribution of contents. The WTO Agreement on TRIPS, which came into effect on 1 January 1995, is the most comprehensive multi-lateral agreement on intellectual property.

The areas of intellectual property covered by TRIPS include copyright and related rights (i.e. the rights of performers, producers of sound recordings and broadcasting organizations), trademarks (including service marks), geographical indications (including appellations of origin), industrial designs, patents (including the protection of new varieties of plants), the layout designs of integrated circuits and undisclosed information (including trade secrets and test data).

The international debate on copyright issues in a digital era also led to the adoption in 1996 of the "WIPO Internet Treaties", which entered into force in 2002. The common objectives of these treaties are to protect copyright owners in the digital age, favour the development of human creativity and promote electronic commerce.

The adoption of the TRIPS and WIPO Internet treaties has influenced the adoption by developed and developing countries of national legislation in line with the principles set forth by the two treaties. For example, in adopting the Digital Millennium Copyright Act (DMCA), the United States updated its copyright law for the digital era and prepared itself for the ratification of the WIPO Internet treaties.

The DMCA included provisions concerning the circumvention of copyright protection systems, fair use in a digital environment, and online service provider (OSP) liability. Moreover, the IIPA is responsible for tracking developments in the area of copyright legislation and enforcement in over 80 countries. In doing so, it determines whether the acts, policies or practices of any foreign country infringe on intellectual property rights or fair and equitable market access for individuals in the United States entitled to intellectual property protection.

The European Union has prepared a European Copyright Directive which was adopted in April 2002 and allows the European Union and its member States to ratify the WIPO Internet Treaties. This is expected to happen by the end of 2002. By 2004, all European countries will need to have adapted their national legislations in order to extend copyright protection to the Internet and other new media in accordance with this Directive.

After many years of legal discussion, to balance the rights of creators and the privacy of users, the Directive offers the possibility for European Union member States to adopt all or part of copyright exceptions that it envisages would allow for copying for technical reasons, personal use and archival purposes. Modernizing the traditional legal instruments of multilateral copyright conventions and treaties is essential, but the costs and benefits of harmonization are not always equally shared. Indeed, developing countries lag behind in terms of producing intellectual property as a whole, including published materials. However, this should not draw attention from the benefits that developing countries stand to gain from ratifying and enforcing copyright legislation.

The adoption of the WIPO treaties in 1996 generated an international pressure on developed and developing countries to comply with international agreements and thus, enforce anti-piracy mechanisms with regard to imported products. Indeed, the recent flurry of implementation of copyright legislation at the national level responds to pressure exerted on Governments by international bodies and local industries to provide effective enforcement of these laws.

As part of WIPO's and WTO's joint efforts to help developing countries meet their commitments regarding intellectual property and conform with the WTO agreement on TRIPS, since 1998 technical assistance in preparing legislation, training, institution building, and modernizing intellectual property systems and enforcement has been extended to developing countries.

National legislation has been enacted by the majority of countries worldwide to ensure copyright protection in the digital age, but it is too early to assess the effectiveness of these actions. While software and music piracy remain the most important economic issues for all countries, other works, such as books, are also under threat as advances in digital technologies facilitate the expansion of piracy.

In one of its country reports, the IIPA indicates that piracy "is rapidly changing: it is becoming more predominantly digital, moving online, and migrating to dispersed production formats such as CD-Recordable (CDR). Piracy of analog formats - audiocassettes, videocassettes, and books and other printed materials - remains a serious, and in some instances a worsening, problem. But technological and market trends are clearly pushing piracy in a new direction. Simply put, technological advances are increasing the opportunities for piracy, and pirates are taking full advantage of them."

All countries, including developing ones, are urged to comply with international agreements to protect works from piracy for the benefit of exporters of intellectual property products. However, enforcement of intellectual property rights depends on the effective functioning of a country's judicial system.

Beyond legal solutions and actions carried out by the local police, prevention campaigns have recently been launched by developing countries to demonstrate their commitment to fighting copyright infringement. Creating awareness of intellectual property rights, including copyright issues, has for the past few years been the preoccupation of intellectual property and copyright offices both in developed and developing countries. The advent of new technologies has spurred a large number of countries to reform their national copyright law in order to ensure copyright protection for materials available over the Internet.

However, bringing copyright laws into line with the WTO Agreement's and WIPO treaties, and providing effective enforcement of these laws with regard to piracy, counterfeiting and other forms of intellectual property rights infringement has proved to be difficult.

Due to the complexity of intellectual property laws and their enforcement, developing countries still lag behind and have still not managed to comply with the TRIPS requirements and enforcement mechanisms. Priority must be given to the development of a policy framework that allows great flexibility while ensuring implementation of international agreements.

The following are some key questions relating to business models and strategies to be considered. They are outlined here to provide a guide and an indication of the scope of the work involved and the types of investments to be made.

Strategies for prospective publishers and authors:

(a) As e-publishing demands new skills, publishers would need to take measures to train staff members to use new technologies, especially in areas that do not exist in traditional print publishing, such as interactivity and multimedia capability etc. One option is to contract out the technical tasks to technology firms or established e-publishers. If the publishing is to be undertaken in-house, an analysis of the capital and operating costs associated with the required information technology and infrastructure needs to be undertaken.

(b) Where a publisher is a start-up firm with no existing investment in print publishing, there appears to be a widely held view that such a venture should commence on an electronic-only basis, although this is feasible only where the majority of readers have Internet access. The question is more complex for publishers that have invested in print publishing. The "parallel" model of print publishing combined with electronic publishing appears to be the most prevalent. The decision essentially involves weighing costs against marketing opportunities. The publisher needs to assess the expenditure costs of converting from print publishing to electronic-only publishing and compare them with the expected gains. On the marketing side, if most users can only access print publications (as would be the case in most developing countries), a move to electronic-only publishing may entail a total loss of market.

(c) Other questions that would need to be addressed include the following:.

(i) Whether to establish on one's own website or be hosted by other sites;

(ii) What kinds of materials are suitable for e-publishing;

(iii) Whether to place online the full text, only the table of contents, or only selected chapters;

(iv) Which distribution channels to use, including institutional buyers (libraries), wholesale and retail stores, specialist document delivery services, etc. A decision also has to be made whether a publication should be delivered online or through a portable device such as a CDROM. A CDROM may be the better option in developing countries where Internet connectivity is still poor, although the trend is now towards online publishing, and a CDROM cannot be updated or easily link readers to Internet sites. E-publishing on CDROM should therefore be considered a transitional stage. Online delivery can occur via optical disk systems through public network connections (ISDN) or directly over the Internet. The publisher has various options regarding the format or language to be used, including ASCII, HTML and PDF. There are also options with regard to the graphic and audiovisual tools to be used. These choices require a fair amount of knowledge about IT and should also take into account trends in languages used on the Internet in order to ensure compatibility.

(v) Whether to build own databases as a backup information source;

(vi) Whether to "bundle" books or journals -that is sell them as a package;

(vii) Which pricing models to use;

(viii) How many of the value-added features enabled by e-publishing (e.g. searching capability, multimedia) are to be provided, taking into account the costs involved and the market being targeted;

(ix) How the publication should be marketed;

(x) Undertaking copyright, ISBN and other registrations;

(xi) How to obtain editorial services;

(xii) Whether the publisher should cooperate with other publishers to gain economies of scale, a factor that has driven some major publishers into mergers and acquisitions; and

(xiii) Whether an author should engage in self-publishing and what external support is available for this purpose.

A number of guidelines for e-publishing dealing with these types of questions and more technical ones are available and may be consulted.

Strategies for users of e-publications

Users include individual buyers of publications and institutional buyers, essentially libraries of different types. Usually publishers negotiate deals when issuing licenses for publications such as journals to libraries. These arrangements specify prices for various print and electronic versions. A library has to weigh cost against the importance it attaches to print relative to electronic versions for reasons other than cost.

Given fixed budgets, when adopting e-publications users may have to choose not merely between print and electronic versions but also between different types of publications - for example, between e-books and e-journals to the extent that there is scope for substitution between them. In their purchasing and other operational activities, libraries may create or join library consortia in order to gain bargaining power vis-à- vis publishers. Such consortia are now being used widely at the national, regional and international levels. Their functions include selecting electronic publishing resources and entering into licensing arrangements with publishers in order to rationalize price negotiations.

Members monitor the market for publications, obtain offers and evaluate them for negotiating purposes. Collaboration between consortia members also extends to providing joint access to acquired e-publications, which is the equivalent of interlibrary loans for print publications. If a group of libraries wishes to establish a consortium, there are published guidelines that provide information on how to create such an institution. Libraries may also join existing consortia such as the International Coalition of Library Consortia (ICOLC), which has worldwide membership.

There are a number of other possible strategies for institutional users. For example, while not many titles may currently be available as e-books, such books provide a cost-effective solution to libraries' budgetary constraints in that a library owning an e-book may transfer the content into several readers' e-book devices and thus avoid purchasing several copies of the same book.

E-books may also help libraries reduce the delays typically involved in interlibrary loans of printed books - a library can obtain the contents of an e-book from another library in a matter of minutes. However, a decision to purchase e-books format has to take into consideration the present and projected availability of needed titles in e-books and the suitability of the available technology for reading books, as well as its cost.

Role of governments

Most developing countries have traditionally printed many types of official documents. Because of high printing and distribution costs, such documents are usually distributed only within government circles and to a few external outlets.

Most governments and government- related institutions in developing countries now have websites or at least make use of other web-sites and portals to publish various types of information. This means that there is scope for governments to provide their publications online.

An expansion of electronic publications by governments would not only widen the distribution of vital government information, it would also provide leadership by example to authors and publishers in the private sector.

To promote e-publishing, some governments in both developed and developing countries have encouraged all government institutions to progressively adopt e-publishing. Some governments have established minimum standards for government e-publications. These standards are intended to ensure the quality and accessibility of the published information. Developing countries should find these examples a useful guide in establishing their own protocols.

6

Digital Trends

Progress in new technology and its speedy development has resulted in many new applications such as multimedia products and services, and 'intelligent' interfaces. These new possibilities, which began in industrialized countries, have gradually spread around the world and offer new opportunities for distance learning, health and many other activities designed for development. Access to knowledge and information via new networks can be a positive contribution to the sustainable development of different sectors of society.

The question, however, is how to apply the new information and communication technologies effectively to development and how to use them in order to bridge the gap between the rich and the excluded, between nations and within those selfsame nations. The question stems from the heated debate between researchers and communication professionals about the conditions for transferring new information and communication technology to developing countries. A certain number, the advocates of the 'modernization paradigm', consider that the transfer of new information and communication technology is a major stimulant for the development process that, in the long run, will enable the developing countries to catch up with the industrialized countries. For others, the opponents of 'cultural dependence', any such transfer would merely be a step further not only towards inequality, but even towards the destruction of the cultural identity of societies in the Southern hemisphere. Finally, for others again, both the paradigms of transfer and dependence are outdated.

New information and communication technology and its applications provide developing countries with the ability to perform a kind of 'technological leapfrogging' that could enable them to reach the connection capacity required for the information networks far more rapidly. Similar forms of leapfrogging might also enable economies with a high level of skilled labour to switch to 'value-added' economies. An increasing number of states share the latter point of view and have opted for the most advanced forms of technology to implement or renew their communication infrastructures.

On the one hand they have adopted policies of adaptation and technological transfer by offering attractive subcontracting capabilities, thereby relocating communication multinationals; on the other hand, they are investing in communication programmes or setting up new communication infrastructures. Other countries, particularly in South-East Asia, have achieved something of a feat in telecommunications and the audiovisual field. Some of these nations even form the driving force for economic expansion that counterbalances the climate of recession elsewhere in the world. South-East Asia currently enjoys the highest rate of economic growth worldwide and operates as an accelerator for the whole continent: 11 per cent per year since 1983 compared with a global growth rate of 6 per cent. Its telecommunication equipment population is now close to that of the industrialized countries and in some areas is even a length ahead of European states.

China, India and several countries in South-East Asia have launched their own satellites. Nevertheless, it would probably be a mistake to think that all developing countries could automatically attain this level of development. The countries in this region of the world find themselves in widely differing economic situations as a result of a series of factors, the most important of which are the ability to attract investment, the educational level of the population, the economic policies adopted by their leaders and, finally, their cooperation with the industrialized countries and the impact of all these factors on new information and communication technology and its applications.

In fact, most of the developing countries are confronted with economic and political alternatives of a strategic nature, but also with constraints and obstacles that they will have to overcome or manage if in the future they wish to set up gateways with the networks and services promised by the information society. These obstacles are financial, technical and political in nature. First and foremost, the introduction of new information and communication technology requires extremely heavy investment, estimated at several hundred billion dollars, a sum that most developing countries can neither raise nor commit.

In addition, most of these states are currently confronted with obstacles to development and are subject to structural adjustment plans that force them to limit their expenditure. Second, the hypothetical presence of these countries on the future electronic networks presupposes the installation of terrestrial or satellite telecommunication networks, the management and control of which seem incompatible with the obsolete and under-equipped level of local telecommunication services.

Third, the future information society presupposes fair, universal access to the Web for the whole population of a country. The geographical dissimilarities within these countries, however, are alarming. They stem from the political options that have been adopted by governments which are generally centralizing in outlook, resulting in fairly top-heavy media concentration, with telecommunication services located in the capitals and major provincial capitals Together, those problems and obstacles clearly illustrate the challenges that the developing countries must face: implementing a new information and communication policy in order to modernize, democratize and diversify the services on offer. The first of these challenges entails favouring a worldwide strategy for the reform of communication services.

The need to modernize communication equipment presupposes the transfer of the new technology and intensive use of the services it provides. The funds required, however, are such that modernization inevitably entails monopoly deregulation, a fact which has now become the reference framework for any upgrade or modernization of communication policy. Most developing countries are fully aware of this need, and have already opted for deregulation or privatization by having their companies join the trend of internationalization and partnerships with the major operators in the industrialised countries. Without subscribing to some form of liberal economic determinism, privatization can probably solve a number of requirements, including that of providing the specific value-added services necessary for any connection with telecommunications networks.

On the other hand, privatization can be seen as a legitimate means of socioeconomic change only if every class of society gains some benefit from it. This is precisely the reason why privatization must be accompanied by a statutory framework guaranteeing that all sectors of the population, in particular those people living farthest from the major cities, have access to the basic information and communication services, just as, through partnerships or alliances, it should facilitate access to every form of information and communication flow, whether by telephone, audiovisual programmes, the written press, etc.

Finally, the success of privatization presupposes the existence of an open market, strong local enterprise, and fair market rules and regulations to counterbalance the risk, inherent to privatization, of the emergence of new monopolies. The second of the challenges mentioned above is linked to the conditions in which access is gained to technology and to its content. Most developing countries have modest, even outdated telephone services and audiovisual equipment, which cannot easily be adapted to the digital transmission used by electronic networks.

The experts take the view that this deficiency can be made up by satellite technology which will complement the existing terrestrial cellular telephony systems and transport large amounts of data at low cost. The system of transmission by satellite seems to offer several advantages, notably that of covering vast areas and reaching populations in regions with difficult terrain and hostile climates that cannot be covered. Satellites make it possible to broadcast educational and cultural programmes and distance learning courses throughout a country, and finally to connect up to electronic networks.

Since the technical capabilities and possibilities of planetary networks, the most well-known of which is the Internet, seem closest to the idea of open, limitless communication. It is also a practical, economical solution for developing countries if they wish to have access to a universal system of communication that can make good a number of deficiencies, notably in terms of point-to-point communication.

The capability of developing countries to adopt an overall strategy that links the transfer of information and communication technology to a training and research policy. Access to know-how and training in every country is a major priority. The acquisition of know-how and knowledge, which today fill the role played first by landownership and later by capital in transforming modern society, has become a priority in national development strategies.

New information and communication technology is seen as an important means of completing and consolidating the traditional techniques of teaching and learning. Virtually everywhere around the world, development programmes are making increasing use of satellite television, telematics, and even video-conferences in education, health, family planning and community development. The technology permits transmission throughout the national territory of adult training programmes and distance learning courses tailored to suit all kinds of publics.

The technology offers immense possibilities for reaching vast numbers of people, with more efficient and attractive teaching methods than those used in traditional education. In addition to these advantages, if the various costs of training, such as travel in developing countries between badly-serviced rural areas are taken into account, distance learning based on new technology seems particularly cost-effective, and will become even more so as its use develops. In the medical field, new technology such as picture phoning, video-conferences and medical encyclopedias on CD-ROM are responding increasingly to a demand which already exists at the experimental level.

In a few years, doctors, hospitals, laboratories and universities will be networked and capable of telemonitoring diagnoses, analyses and examinations transmitted from one end of the world to the other in record time, via computer and video systems. Examples of experimental applications are already on the increase, notably between hospitals in developed countries.

It is not enough to buy technology to gain access to the information society, however, nor should a straightforward purchase be seen as a miraculous solution. Access entails a considerable degree of effort, information, learning and popularization that developing countries will have to uphold if they wish to benefit from technological change and have the tools necessary for their autonomy, namely new information and communication technology. Nor should the latter be seen as some sort of magic wand far removed from the socioeconomic facts of life of the countries into which they are introduced.

The technology concerns every kind of user: researchers, academics, students, company executives, etc., who have to adapt to their new environment and learn to use their navigation system properly in order to optimize its potential. In addition and in parallel to this, technology transfer has to be supported by a research drive. This consists, first of all, in analysing the breakthroughs made in information technology, the conditions permitting its transfer, and its interaction with the local socioeconomic environment, and discovering the ways in which all these factors occur and interrelate.

The result will be a clearer understanding not only of the use of technology, its effects, and the economic and technical constraints, but also of its advantages and the room for manoeuvre in its application. Within this global framework, research can provide a genuine form of 'strategic surveillance' used to guide policy-making by developing countries with respect to technological options. Research is also a prerequisite for development which is often put to one side by countries that are consumers of new technology.

Many developing countries since their independence have built highly diversified industrial tools in the field of communication systems, while remaining technologically dependent on supplier countries. They often find themselves confronted with R&D issues designed, driven and developed in industrialized countries. The latter have taken the high ground in the field of new technology—or are seeking to do so - by developing scientific research, taking the view that the capability to appropriate and assimilate technology depends on the degree of mastery and development attained in the strategic sector of research and development, a branch of activity in which the most advanced countries have dominant positions.

The issue of international co-operation in the field of communication. The balance sheet, after several decades of international co-operation for development purposes, is disappointing. On the one hand, it shows that very few countries have entered the newly industrialized country category, and that the use of traditional methods of development aid to enhance economic growth must be re-examined. The efforts made by the international community must be upheld and widened to include other underprivileged regions around the world, through a different approach to co-operation.

In concerted fashion, this must include international organizations in order to facilitate partnership agreements with the private sector, include professional skills and ensure marketing and management know-how, and enhance understanding and knowledge with respect to the new legislation on the independent written press and the audiovisual field—in short, a different conception of co-operation altogether, leading to an authentic transfer of knowledge, in a spirit of balanced interests, solidarity and sharing.

ICTs and Digital Divide

ICT is not just another sector of economic development, nor can it simply be looked upon as a set of tools. Instead, ICT permeates every aspect of today's societal activity. Ironically, the very factors that have phenomenally improved productivity by intelligent use of the technology, also risk driving the poor to the periphery, thus creating barriers within and between societies, and could lead to social unrest and tension. Countries and people lacking capacity for ICT will be marginalized in the new economy. New trade barriers will be erected. Moreover, without access to ICT, countries will not be able to benefit from the many innovative ways of addressing poverty and basic needs that these technologies offer.

One reason why the information gap is widening is that the potential of ICT in social and economic development has not been fully understood. There are still too many people in key positions in governments and aid agencies who seem to believe that only when basic needs are met does technology have a role to play. If they were right most of the poor would have to wait forever. The debate must move beyond choosing between ICT and other development needs such as health and education. The issue is not about a trade-off between one or the other, but an understanding that these must go hand in hand. However, technology alone is not enough. Technology must be applied within its social context and that, in many countries, is providing a real challenge. One thing is clear. The new technologies, notably ICT, will bring about major transformations in society.

The structural logic of the information society will be vastly different from that of the industrial society. One eminent scholar, who has given a lot of thought to the implications of the ICT revolution, is Professor Harlan Cleveland. Here is how he perceives the future: "Information -symbols, not things -will be playing the lead role in world history that physical labour, stone, bronze, land, minerals, metals and energy once played. We will have to burn into our consciousness how very different information is from all its predecessors as civilization's dominant resource." In his speech to the American Association for History and Computing Cleveland continues: "Information expands as it's used-no "limits to growth "around here. It is ready transportable, at close to the speed of light.

Information leaks so easily that it is much harder to hide and to hoard than tangible resources were. The spread of knowledge empowers the many, by eroding the influence that once empowered the few who were "in the know". Information cannot be owned, only its delivery service can. And giving or selling information don't give rise to "exchange" transactions; they are acts of sharing." If Cleveland is right, we are at the doorstep of a democratic revolution. In the industrial era, poverty was explained and justified by shortages of things. In the coming years, physical resources will still be important, but their role in wealth creation will gradually be overtaken by information.

And since each baby is born with a brain, there ought to be radically different prerequisites for development and progress at the level of the individual, also in the poor regions of the world. But there is a catch: whether or not the information revolution is really going to lead to greater fairness depends to what extent the poor will have access, not only to the modern information technologies, but also to education. If such access is not provided, the expected fairness revolution will be turned into its opposite.

In February 2001, well above 400 million people worldwide were users of the Internet. This represents phenomenal growth, given that the Internet is less than three thousand days old. But the spread of Internet use is very uneven. The vast majority of Internet users are found in OECD countries. There are more hosts in Manhattan than in continental Africa; more hosts in Finland than in Latin America and the Caribbean; and notwithstanding the remarkable progress in the application of ICT in India, most of its villages still lack a working telephone. To bridge the digital divide is both a moral and a social imperative. If we do not succeed, entire regions and hundreds of millions of people will be left behind. The consequences in terms of poverty and deprivation will be devastating.

But there is another, equally compelling argument for developing countries to embrace the new technologies. By investing in cutting-edge technology, through leapfrogging, they will be able to bypass certain stages of development. The benefits can be financial, social, as well as environmental. As "late-comers", developing countries can be better placed to take advantage of the newest technology developments, not the least in ICT, since they are not hindered by the previous investments in obsolete technology. Since prices come down very quickly in the area of ICT, investments in a telecommunication infrastructure today may cost just a fourth or a fifth compared to what was the case a few years ago.

The environmental benefits would be significant, since leapfrogging would make it possible for developing countries to avoid repeating some of the mistakes of industrialized countries. Take energy. Worldwide total energy production-related investments for 2000 to 2030 are estimated at between 12 and 17 trillion dollars. The majority of these investments will be made in developing countries. Presently, most of them will favour fossil fuels, primarily coal. If this trend continues, the resulting emissions in terms of carbon will be disastrous. And these emissions will negatively affect people all over the world.

New systems of energy supply and consumption are badly needed. Less polluting and more efficient energy technologies are available, but normally at a higher investment cost than conventional fuels. The challenge is at least twofold:

i) to help build the necessary capacity in terms of institutions and skills in developing countries to enable them to adapt and expand on new discoveries and make them applicable to their specific needs, and

ii) to provide investors with the right kind of incentives to make investing in alternative energy solutions attractive.

Only if these preconditions are fulfilled will leapfrogging be possible. Investing in clean energy and transport are the most obvious examples of how the natural environment in developing countries could benefit from technology leapfrogging. But the opportunities do not stop there.

The ICT revolution by itself offers fascinating possibilities for enhancing energy and resource efficiency and reducing pollution. When society becomes more digital, the possibilities for major structural change and efficiency gains multiply. New avenues open up. Concepts such as dematerialisation, teleworking, tele-conferencing, distance education, the flexible office, e-Commerce all promise great leaps forward in terms of enhanced resource efficiency. Environmentally sound technologies (ESTs) often depend on sophisticated measuring devices, data transmission networks and automatic data processing equipment. This can be provided by ICT, thus bringing about more efficient production processes as well as greatly enhanced product performance.

Moreover, with advanced communications many conventional products will be transformed into services. A newspaper becomes an on-line news service; an instruction manual becomes an interactive technical advice service; cinema film reproduction becomes a "video-on-demand "service in the home, etc.

It .appears obvious to us that a high-tech economy based on knowledge, skills and innovation ought to be a cleaner, greener economy. But few attempts have been made to assess specifically to what extent the digital revolution and the sustainable development agenda complement each other.

In some areas developments so far have been disappointing. For instance, as long as e-Commerce is a marginal phenomenon in society, demand for transportation seems to increase, not the opposite. When more and more people will shop on the Net, things will change. The main reason is economics. When volumes increase it will be good business to organize transport and logistics in the most efficient way. As a result the environment will benefit.

The reader may find that most of what ICT can offer in terms of enhanced energy and resource efficiency are relevant examples only in the context of OECD countries. Activities such as telework, e-Commerce, on-line services were pioneered in the US, Japan and Europe. But there is no reason why such activities should not start penetrating countries of the South as well. In fact, they already have.

Many people do not realize that China is the single biggest market for mobile phones in the world today. As the volume of foreign direct investments in developing countries has multiplied in recent years, the result will be an increased transfer of high-tech from OECD countries to developing countries. True, private investments in the South are concentrated to a limited number of countries. The challenge is to include more countries in this process, and to focus specifically on applications that would promote sustainable development.

Traditionally it was accepted that economic growth, as measured by GDP, was inevitably linked to growing demand for raw materials and energy as well as the negative consequences of pollution. If such linkages were to last long into the future the overall consequences for mankind would be disastrous.

There are already clear signs that pollution levels are exceeding the absorption capacity of the global ecosystem. Climate change is the most obvious example but there are others. Parallel to excessive pollution levels, the pressures on forests, farmland, fresh water resources and fisheries are mounting. Efforts to try to de-link GDP growth and demand for energy and materials have therefore become a priority for policymakers in several OECD countries.

The achievements are still limited, but there are signs of progress. For instance, the energy intensity of OECD countries has been reduced in the recent past. This is the result of a shift towards more energy-efficient technologies and less energy-intensive materials. Scientists claim that this trend will continue, as a gradual saturation of traditional consumer goods will take place. One obvious reason is the move into the information economy. In such an economy an increasing part of transactions will be immaterial. Many products will be turned into services, which depend less on energy and material throughput.

Long-term studies of energy-intensity in several countries indicate that economies use more energy per unit of output during the early phases of development, reach a peak, and then start to decrease. Liberalization and information technologies should allow knowledge to be transferred more easily, enabling emerging economies to climb the so-called energy and technology ladders more quickly. This means that latecomers ought to be able to avoid the peak in energy demand by benefiting from more modern methods of manufacturing and more efficient energy technologies. However, there are many barriers to overcome for such change to happen. Studies do confirm that energy intensity is on the increase in most developing countries, not the opposite. The only exception is China, where deliberate efforts are being made to use both energy and materials more efficiently.

In order for the necessary transformation to more efficient and environmentally sound technologies to happen in developing countries, several barriers to change have to be tackled. Most important is to address the capacity needs. While much knowledge for improved problem-solving is now available in many scientific and engineering institutions around the world, very little of that know-how is geared specifically to addressing development and environment needs in developing countries. Most of these countries lack the scientific institutions and infrastructure to adapt and expand on new knowledge and discoveries in order to make them applicable to their local needs.

We are dealing with capital-intensive infrastructure, which is meant to provide a public service at an affordable price. In most countries energy distribution, public transport, waste management etc. are considered to be public services. Increasingly, public authorities are choosing to delegate the operation and management of public services to the private sector. If and when this happens, it is crucial that the necessary regulatory framework is in place to guarantee environmental quality.

To create an adequate legislative and regulatory framework for the protection of the environment is a difficult process in any country. This is particularly true for most developing countries, where government structures are weak. Governments need to implement fiscal and regulatory policies that encourage innovation and provide direct incentives to companies that develop or disseminate technologies that contribute to sustainable development.

Fiscal incentives should also be used to stimulate businesses and households to purchase such technologies. Parallel to that, subsidies in support of fossil fuels and other technologies that are harmful to the environment should be dismantled. The next step would be for governments to apply the Polluter Pays Principle, i.e. to make sure that environmental externalities are reflected in market prices. This represents a real challenge in OECD countries, and even more so in developing countries, but it has to happen.

As already stressed, the strengthening of institutional and human capacities is a primary prerequisite for ESTs to become a priority in the development process of developing countries. The same is true for most development co-operation agencies. In a recent study on "Technology co-operation in the field of environmentally sound technologies "to the European Parliament by IED the authors conclude that "a review of organisational structures and portfolios of bilateral and multilateral co-operation agencies and banks shows that there are grossly insufficient human capacities in the areas of energy co-operation. If ESTs are to become a priority of development co-operation, the institutions of international co-operation must first and foremost be given the means to understand the issues and to formulate and manage projects ".

Until recently, science and technology was more or less absent from the sustainable development debate. More recently a change can be discerned. The Human Development Report 2001 "Making New Technologies Work for Human Development "is one example. The report emphasizes the crucial relationship that exists between science, knowledge and human capacity in addressing issues of sustainable development. One important message from the Human Development Report is that technological progress and knowledge applications are key drivers of economic growth. The logical conclusion is that support to science and technology ought to become a top priority for development co-operation.

The little attention given by ODA, so far, to science and technology also means that support to ESTs have been largely neglected. The only mechanism at international level worth mentioning in this context is the Global Environment Facility (GEF). The GEF has given support to capacity building in the field of sustainable energy and to renewable energy pilot projects. But compared to the total investments in energy production in developing countries, the resources of the GEF have been woefully inadequate.

One possible source of finance, that ought to be utilised in support of investments in ESTs, is the export-credit agencies (ECAs) of OECD countries. However, until very recently these agencies were paying no attention at all to the environmental aspects of their lending. On the contrary, during the period of 1994-99, it is estimated that more than 100 billion of US dollars were being mobilised through the ECAs in support of investments in carbon-based technologies. Just imagine if the same attention had been given instead to investments in energy efficiency and renewables.

Efforts have been made within the climate convention to establish new sources of finance to assist developing countries both in climate adaptation and investments in clean technologies. It is too early today to judge to what extent the new mechanisms will make a difference.

Presently, we experience the technologies of the information and communication revolution at the cutting edge of progress. Their application also offers momentous opportunities for development. They present developing countries with real opportunities in helping to bridge the economic and prosperity gaps between them and developed countries.

Today, village computer centers in developing countries help farmers check the going prices for their produce in the city, thus avoiding arbitrary mark-ups by middlemen. The same centers provide distance education and learning and help improve health services. Today, rural artists and craftsmen in remote villages can reach a global market with their products, thanks to non-profit

Internet sites. Yet, at the same time, billions of people still live untouched by the digital revolution. Only about 7% of the world 's population can claim connectivity, and the greater majority of these are living in the developed countries. As a result, the income gap between the developed and developing countries is being further aggravated by the digital divide.

This holds ominous consequences for the developing countries in terms of increased poverty, unemployment and underdevelopment. This is not the result of some conspiracy against the poor. Rather it is the result of a development where access to information and knowledge are becoming the most important factors of production. Those with access to information and technology naturally benefit in this situation; those without access become further marginalized.

However, the situation should not be regarded as hopeless. Even if the information revolution so far is widening the gap between the rich and the poor, this need not become a pattern for the future. There are many tangible examples from around the world of how ICTs are being deployed to address important development goals. Evidence shows that ICT initiatives need not be confined to countries with high per capita incomes, well-developed infrastructures and high levels of venture capital in order to succeed. Indeed, remarkable progress is evident where some of these elements have been lacking. The experiences of a few countries, including both developing countries and transition economies, have demonstrated that bold actions in bringing their countries into the digital age have paid off and brought tangible results in economic, social and political terms. Prominent examples are Estonia, Mauritius and Costa Rica.

Costa Rica attributes much of its recent economic growth to the widespread adaptation of ICT. The focus has been on the educational sector. Computer laboratories were installed in all of the country's public high schools, thereby reaching 50 per cent of the children enrolled in public schools. "Smart cards" have been introduced nationwide in public administration, transportation, public telephones and health services. Parallel to that a variety of efforts have been made to use ICT to help integrate isolated rural populations, notably by introducing multipurpose/multimedia mobile units that can be taken to any rural community and provide a variety of functions (Internet access, ICT training, e-mail facilities etc.).

Today, the country has one of the highest degrees of connectivity in Europe. All schools have been connected to the Internet; more than 80 per cent of bank transfers are made over the Internet; "smart cards" were introduced for interaction with government services etc. The per capita income has risen from US 600 in 1991 to more than US 5000 in 2000, a development largely made possible by the very proactive ICT strategy pursued. Mauritius adopted a National Information Technology Strategy Plan early on. The primary objectives were to bring Government closer to the people through e-Government, to use ICT to enhance the education system and the service sector, and to improve the efficiency of the public sector. A special Ministry was created to promote ICT applications in different sectors of the Mauritian society. As a result of the dedicated efforts Mauritius has attracted a great number of small and medium-sized ICT-based companies.

The great majority of developing countries, however, have done little in terms of a coherent strategy to embrace the ICT revolution. This does not mean that nothing is happening in all these countries in terms of ICT for development. There are numerous initiatives, mainly among NGOs, that hopefully will help raise awareness and demonstrate, to governments as well as aid agencies, the great opportunities that the new technologies offer both for accelerating economic development and, more specifically, to help advance the human development agenda.

Among the many examples of initiatives at the grassroots level, the following may provide an illustration of the significance of ICT in addressing basic human needs:

The overall aim of the Technology Community Centres Access (TACC) pilot project -established with support of UNDP was to "provide rural and remote communities with public access to information technology, especially the Internet, and with the training to utilize it effectively." The project's ultimate goal was to demonstrate how information technologies could contribute to "the empowerment of community members" and how such technologies could be used "for a variety of applications benefiting sustainable human development." A pilot, consisting of several cyber cafes, was established in Sharkeya.

The pilot has succeeded beyond the most optimistic expectations. Some 6,000 persons have received IT training with a view to supporting various development activities at the community level. To date, TACC staff - national and international (mainly United Nations 'Volunteers)-have developed and posted over 1,000 web pages, most of them in Arabic. The websites provide information on ICT training, health, agriculture, e-commerce, the culture and history of Egypt, recreational activities, etc.

In light of the success in Sharkeya, the government of Egypt recently decided to establish similar centers in all of the country 's Governorates. The TACC concept is also being replicated in Jordan.

The experimental telecentre project in South India was initiated in 1998 by the M.S.Swaminathan Research Foundation. Four centers have become operational, located in villages with illiteracy rates above 50%. The project is based on the understanding that networked information requires "mediation "by professionals if it is to be accessible to poor rural villagers. The information compiled and collected for the project is primarily based on requests by the village end-users. This information - which includes items like commodity prices, weather forecasts, daily news, government information, methods of dealing with crop diseases, fishing methods etc.-is translated into Tamil, packaged into audio files and distributed via the Internet to the four Village Knowledge Centres. The local centers broadcast the audio files over loudspeakers to the illiterate villagers. Evidence suggests that the villagers benefit significantly from the information in regard to making decisions affecting their lives and well-being.

Women members of Grameen Bank are offered micro-credit loans to purchase cellular phones, which are subsequently rented out to village farmers and other community members. As of July 2001 phones had been placed in more than 1.000 villages. Phone services in rural areas are highly valued in Bangladesh and have rapidly increased incomes and savings among phone owners. The village phones allow family members to stay in touch and communicate with family members abroad about financial matters like remittances. Local farmers use the phones to have access to market information, weather reports and pest alerts. The phone services have also contributed to improvements in disaster response, crime rates and livestock mortality through better access to public services.

The association of Uganda Women Medical Doctors was started in 1987 with a mission of improving and facilitating the promotion and protection of health to women, young people and children in Uganda. They decided in the spring of 2000 to try to make use of Internet in their work. The aim of the project was to disseminate information on reproductive health electronically to other women NGOs. Medical doctors in Kampala download the necessary information, repackage it and send it online to the participating NGOs. Feedback from the NGOs is also received via the Internet, including specific questions asked by clients at health clinics. Already after a few months the project had demonstrated increased awareness among rural women of reproductive health issues.

A fascinating pilot project in the field of ICT for development is currently being developed by Development Alternatives, Delhi. The main objective of TARAhaat (Technology and Action for Rural Advancement)—the Internet Portal connecting rural India to the global village -is to use the power of ICT to bring knowledge, services and products to the villages in India. Starting in Punjab and Uttar Pradesh, the plan is to establish tens of thousands of Internet and computer enabled business centers all over the subcontinent in the years to come.

The portal offers email, eCommerce, education, entertainment, access to e-Government facilities, etc. Eventually TARAhaat plans to bring the village manufacturers in contact with buyers and designers the world over. Access to the portal is being provided by franchised cyber kiosks, which are operated by local village entrepreneurs. Satellite communication, wireless broadband and local power generation will be used where there is no electricity or phone. Overall few donor-funded ICT projects in developing countries have proven to be self-sustaining once external assistance has run out.

The encouraging thing about TARAhaat is that its pilots shows signs of being able to stand on their own feet only after six to twelve months of operation. This means that the revenues generated by these kiosks are sufficiently large to provide a surplus. What this demonstrates is that even in the poorest of villages there is significant demand for communication and ICT services.

In Tanzania, Masai pastoralists living in the Ngorongoro have used the Internet to voice their opposition to Government conservation management policy that threatened their land and their livelihood. A member of the Masai community came up with the idea of putting his people on the World Wide Web after he made a video about the critique of the pastoralists on the Governments management plan for their land. He put clips of "real people" from the video to the website and managed to mobilize support for the cause of the pastoralists around the world. In addition to obliging the Tanzanian Government to listen to the voices of the local communities, the Masai say that their web site makes them feel less isolated: they feel part of a "bigger world".

ICT has been extremely beneficial for those nations that have used it with determination and enthusiasm as part of their national development strategies. Many individual examples from developing countries also demonstrate how ICT, appropriately applied, can help address basic social needs. In spite of this, the international donor community has been slow in addressing the digital divide. There has been much talk but little action. At the receiving end, there has also been a lot of resistance. Quite a number of developing country governments have been slow to open up to ICT, either for political or cultural reasons, or simply because they do not believe that ICT can be of importance to the development of their countries.

If the general trend among donors can be characterized as passivity, a few institutions have understood the importance of ICT for development. Canadian IDRC has been a strong promoter of ICT capacity building for over a decade. Swedish SAREC also played a supporting role in the early years. The main focus for IDRC and SAREC has been to build capacity for ICT at universities and scientific institutions in the South. IDRC has also been a pioneer in other areas, using ICT in natural resources management, the provision of health care, etc.

ICT for development became a central issue for the World Bank in the mid 1990´s. Jim Wolfensohn had joined the bank as president and soon declared that he wanted to turn the bank into a "knowledge bank." The bank has since launched several good initiatives, like InfoDev and Gateway. Support to ICT capacity building, however, is still far from being among the Bank 's priorities in terms of funding.

The UN system has been a disappointment, mainly because of shrinking funding support for UN agencies in general. There are two exceptions, the ITU and UNDP. The ITU has done its part in terms of awareness-raising activities, but -true to its mandate -focusing mainly on the need for reform and liberalization of the telecommunication sector.

UNDP was a pioneer with its Sustainable Development Networks Programme and its ICT for development project. But the budgetary resources were limited, which meant that activities had to focus on information, awareness-raising activities and pilot projects.

The European Union commands significant resources for development co-operation, in fact significantly larger than the UN. But the European Commission has so far largely neglected the information revolution and its implications for development. This is in stark contrast to the efforts undertaken within the Union itself. The European Commission has taken on a very active role in the promotion of ICT through the launching of eEurope -a broad programme aiming at enhancing ICT skills in society with special efforts made towards public schools, universities, SME:s, people with different kinds of handicaps, etc. One of the main objectives is to make sure that no citizens of the Union are being excluded from the technology developments.

If developments have been slow in the past as regards donor support to ICT for development, however important changes took place during 2000. In this year, major international bodies launched potentially highly significant initiatives to apply ICT to the needs of the developing countries.

The United Nations Millennium Summit called on the UN "to play a leadership and catalytic role in helping to bridge the digital divide and accelerate development by harnessing the development potential of information and communication technologies (ICTs)". A Special Task Force has been established to provide overall leadership in helping "to formulate strategies for ICTs development and putting them at the service of development for all, to forge a strategic partnership between the United Nations system, private industry and financing trusts and foundations, donors, programme countries and other relevant stakeholders, and to mobilize new resources for ICT for development ".

Parallel to the discussions in the UN, the G8 meeting in Okinawa in July 2000 decided to establish two special task forces; one on the digital divide and one on renewable energy. The task forces included members from governments, the private sector, science and civil society. By initiating this work, the major economic powers of the world demonstrated their concern both for the issue of income poverty - access to modern energy services is a precondition for development -and information poverty. The two reports were presented at the G8 meeting in Genoa in July 2001. Both reports are of high quality and include a large number of very sensible recommendations. It is however not at all clear to what extent G8 countries will act upon the recommendations.

Comments in Genoa, notably from Mr.Bush, stressed unequivocally that there was nothing binding about the recommendations. Leaving aside implementation, the two task forces did serve an important function. Their analysis is cutting-edge and they will most certainly be used to advance the agenda in terms of bridging the digital divide as well as promoting environmentally sound technologies in the South.

Professor Jeffrey Sachs has pointed out that the greatest divide between rich and poor nations is the inequality in innovation and diffusion of technology. Even as we speak this divide is widening. Among the solutions, Sachs suggests to follow the example of the Rockefeller Foundation in creating and funding great research centres around the world. New partnerships are also needed to bring together academia, governments and industry, from both rich and poor countries.

Capacity building in the new technology areas at universities, government institutions, schools, among entrepreneurs, etc, is a major prerequisite for technology leapfrogging to become successful. Furthermore, developing countries need considerable help to develop the right political, fiscal and legal frameworks to stimulate investments in ICT as well as ESTs. One of the mistakes of the past was that development co-operation was primarily seen in the context of the governments involved.

But experience has taught us that governments seldom are good at handling and managing technology. This should be the responsibility of the private sector. Hence there is a strong need in developing countries for new types of partnerships between the public and private sectors. This is particularly true in areas like telecom and energy, where rigid state monopolies very often are the main stumbling block for improvements in customer services.

There is no doubt that the economic opportunities which ICT generates will create a lot of wealth for those who master them. However, left entirely to market forces, these technologies are likely to marginalize the poor and disenfranchise them even more.

A purely public sector approach will not work either. What is very much needed are partnerships between the private and public sectors, where the key role of the public sector will be to strengthen the capacity of all major sectors in society to have access to the Internet and to use it for their benefit. The private sector should be responsible for ensuring efficient and commercially viable dissemination of the technologies. Academia and civil society would help develop content so as to address important social, environmental and cultural needs in the process.

Many different kinds of technology can contribute to sustainable development. Some of these may be designed specifically to tackle environmental or poverty-related problems (e.g. solar photovoltaics). However, other technologies that have not been designed to directly address these kind of problems - like computers and mobile phones -will have an equally important role to play.

The technologies needed for sustainable development will differ from country to country. Those best placed to identify their technology needs are the different stakeholders themselves. However, they will only be able to do so if there is a supportive and enabling environment: if they have a well-developed skills base; strong, well-targeted programmes of research and development; an entrepreneurial private sector and if financing is available to the companies that are developing and utilising the technologies.

The private sector will need a lot of support in most developing countries in order to invest in the new technology areas. FDI flows are, as we know, concentrated in a few developing countries. For the great majority of countries the political as well as financial risks are perceived to be too high. Moreover, FDI will not take place in countries were the infrastructure in terms of roads, ports, telecom, energy, etc, is poor. A classic Catch 22 situation. Here the international donor community could play an important role by providing credits and risk guarantees.

Small-scale enterprises and service companies have a key role to play in developing and disseminating technology. Smaller companies in developing countries often experience difficulties to obtain financing. They are either too large for micro-credits, too small to qualify for project financing or perceived as too much of a risk for commercial loans. Strategies for providing funding to small private businesses need to be developed.

The international community should play a central role in assisting development country governments in pursuing the goal of Digital Opportunities for all and to support green technology leapfrogging.

The following priority actions ought to be considered:

— Support to national eStrategies, based on broad stakeholder dialogues. These strategies should include the development of regulatory and policy frameworks so as to improve competition in telecommunications and the provision of IT services to the public.

— Support for the establishment of community access points in all developing countries. The goal should be that all communities in the developing world should be connected before the end of 2004.

— Promotion of ICT dissemination among children in developing countries, notably by connecting schools and educational facilities.To be effective, such a program must be complemented by adequate teacher training.

— Support for university-based centres and research networks, focussing on research and learning at the intersection of ICT and development. Special attention should be given to content building within areas like tele-medicine, distance education, democracy and participation etc.

— Strengthen efforts to mobilize public and private support for improvements of basic ICT infrastructure in developing countries. Sufficient ODA funds -a combination of grants and soft loans -must be raised to cover political and financial risks and to guarantee connectivity in remote areas.

— Support to national strategies for sustainable energy, i.e. strategies based on energy efficiency and renewable.

— Support to capacity building within developing country governments for sustainable energy; the same capacity needs in donor agencies and development banks must also be addressed.

— Before 2010, reduce by half the number of people without access to modern energy services, notably through investments in renewable energy. This would require a crash programme in terms of donor assistance. Priority should be given to small-scale projects that meet local needs, and on leveraging private finance.

— The development of renewables should be strengthened through focussed R&D efforts and public procurement, thereby driving down the costs of ESTs.

- Launching of a special programme to promote renewable energy systems in remote locations to which traditional grid-based infrastructure does not reach. In such locations solar-based systems can be the only cost-effective option. Through such solutions, vital energy needs like lighting, refrigeration, etc, as well as ICT connectivity can be met.
- Encourage the use of Export-Credit Agencies to promote investments in ICT infrastructure as well as in energy efficiency and renewables.
- Make sure that access to modern energy services becomes part of developing country poverty eradication strategies.
- Promoting debt swaps, by making money made available through the HIPC initiative to support the implementation of technology development programmes.
- Promoting new international centres of excellence in research in technologies for sustainable development.

7

Challenges of Online Environment

The Internet consists of a network of computer networks which span the world. The Internet was developed in the 1960's for military purposes, as a decentralised communications system which could survive damage to one part of the network. Decentralisation remains an important characteristic of the Internet. By the 1970s, academics began to use the Internet as the computer networks which had emerged in universities were first linked with networks in other academic institutions and later to the Internet. In recent years there has been a dramatic expansion in Internet usage around the globe with an equally dramatise increase in the amount and range of material available on-line.

Part of the reason for the growth in Internet usage flows from the relatively low costs of participation relative to other media. The necessary equipment comprises a computer, a modem and access to a telephone line, the cost of which is not insignificant but which is within the reach of many individuals and organisations. It is important to note that the Internet did not depend on commercial incentives for its growth. Rather it has developed essentially from a desire to share and obtain information, entertain, and communicate. Many Internet users view themselves as part of an 'Internet community'.

The on-line environment has now become a rapidly expanding international medium in which literally millions of users are providing and accessing content on a daily basis. For this reason the Internet offers unprecedented variety and quantity of content that is continuously changing as content is added, updated and moved around the world. As no single entity controls the operation of the Internet or the material available on it, it is impossible to form a picture at any point in time of what exactly the Internet looks like, its size or the quality or quantity of content available. Content accessible on the Internet is stored in thousands of linked computers and is equally available by and from governments, corporations, interest groups, institutions and individuals from anywhere around the world. At present most of this content is provided free of charge. Whilst material can be accessed from any computer connected to the network, it is important to note that the content may be actually stored on a number of different computers or 'servers', which need not be in the same jurisdiction as the person accessing or creating the material.

In order to understand the nature of the Internet it is useful to identify the functions which are being performed by those who are participating in the medium. These functions include providing content, accessing content, connecting others to the network and/or providing the telecommunications infrastructure. However, it is important to recognise that, unlike traditional broadcasting and publication models where the roles of content providers, publishers and viewers tend to be fairly fixed, the activities being performed by a participant on the Internet often encompass more than one function and many participants perform different functions at different times. Of all the functions being performed in the on-line environment the distinction between 'users' and 'content providers' may be the most blurred. This is because any person or organisation can access and/or add to content available at any time. For example, a person can read and send text to a newsgroup or mailing list, create a web site or browse and retrieve information, all of which may occur in the same Internet session.

Accordingly, drawing a distinction between accessing content and providing content is more a theoretical construct that usefully describes the two separate functions, which are often performed by the same participant in the on-line environment. The term 'user' is generally used to refer to a consumer of on-line services who accesses material available on-line, typically via a link with the network through a service provider. A 'content provider' is described as a person or organisation which provides content in the on-line environment. Content may comprise text, data, still graphics, audio, video, computer programs or a combination of all of these. Organisations and individuals who provide access to on-line services to other users and content providers are referred to as 'service providers'. This incorporates those who merely provide access to the computer network which makes up the Internet, sometimes called 'access providers', as well as those who provide access along with additional services to their clients, such as assisting clients to transform content into an attractive format display on the world wide web, facilitating easy access to new and/or interesting sites and help desk facilities. Service providers range in size from individuals to small businesses, universities, government corporations and multinational organisations with operations in several countries. Service providers usually provide their clients with 'space' to store content, such as web sites, on their computers, which are sometimes called 'servers'. This enables their clients to create and provide Internet content which can be accessed by other Internet users.

Different service providers have different policies regarding the material which their clients provide and store on their servers. Some service providers requiring content providers to meet certain standards, whilst others do not wish to concern themselves with the nature of content at all. Some service providers also temporarily store or 'cache' popular Internet content from remote computers onto their servers in order to facilitate faster and more efficient access to this material for their users. Service providers who provide access to the Internet operate as part of a network of computers. Accordingly, they enable users to access content contained on their own servers, as well as material held on the network of computers which make up the Internet, which may be stored on computers within the country in which the service providers operate, or on other computers around the world.

Due to the vast amounts of Internet content which can be accessed from computers all around the world, along with the fact that Internet content is constantly changing, service providers are often not aware of, and are not in a position to be aware of, most of the material which can be accessed by those who use their service.

Encryption transfers and the use of alternative routes and protocols further exacerbates this issue and renders the blocking of even those sites which have been identified extremely problematic. The network infrastructure necessary to support on-line services in any country is usually provided by telecommunication carriers.

On-line service providers usually lease telephone and data line capacity directly from the network infrastructure providers, or from 'resellers'. The potential uses and opportunities presented by the Internet for enhancing the way we communicate and access information, educational and entertainment resources appear to be unlimited. Some of the major modes of communication presently available on the Internet include e-mail, newsgroups, the World Wide Web, Internet Relay Chat, voice and teleconferencing facilities to name only a few. Each of these services can be used for a wide range of purposes and each uses its own set of technical protocols. Given the extremely dynamic nature of the Internet, it is highly likely that the range and nature of the services available throughout the medium will continue to develop at a rapid rate.

From the time the Internet was first developed it has been used for virtually all forms of communication, from one-to-one communications to one-to-many communications. Forums also exist for group discussions in real time, as well as over time. One of the main methods of communications is Electronic mail, or e-mail as it is widely known. E-mail allows users to send text messages and files to one another via personal computers. Its popularity stems from convenience, speed of delivery and low cost, as well as the capacity to reach millions of people throughout the world. In addition, the ability to transmit files of information in the form of documents, spreadsheets, graphics, sounds and computer programs as attachments to messages makes e-mail a powerful application.

E-mail is increasingly being used as a mainstream form of communication for individuals, governments, educational bodies and industry. E-mail messages are most often used for private communication, as they are addressed to an individual person or group of named individuals. In this respect, e-mail can perform a similar function to letters, faxes and telephone calls. E-mail messages can also be sent to groups of people who are members of mailing lists. These lists are usually maintained on specific computers to which individuals can subscribe by submitting their e-mail addresses. While some mailing lists are not controlled in any way, others are supervised in that each message sent to the list is reviewed by a moderator who then decides whether to allow the message to be sent on to members. Similarly, the acceptance of new members to a list may be controlled by a moderator. An e-mail can also serve as a form of identification when a person subscribes to additional services or seeks to access content from other computers. However, it is important to note that e-mail addresses need not reflect the actual name of any given person or organisation and a person may have several e-mail addresses and/or use pseudonyms or aliases in their on-line communications.

Usenet 'newsgroups' are another popular mode of communication. The term 'newsgroups' generally refers to a world wide distributed system of discussion fora. Fora have been set up on virtually every topic imaginable and users whose service provider subscribes to a particular 'newsgroup' can access and participate in these open group discussions. Messages are posted onto news servers which are distributed to other news servers around the world. Content providers may identify themselves or participate anonymously. Content providers can also communicate with a wide audience by establishing a web site on which they can display text, graphics, or provide video, audio services and software. The ability to use these modes of communication to reach a potentially international audience is one of the most important aspects of the Internet. It has the potential to enhance social and political participation of individuals and enable the exchange of ideas across geographic and political boundaries.

The Internet's capacity as an educational and cultural resource is enormous. Via the Internet users can access data bases, texts, journals, articles, reports, state documents, encyclopedias and legislation which are held by public and university libraries, government departments and organisations around the world. Many art galleries, museums and cultural institutions have also established web sites containing images and information about works in their collections, providing an enormous amount of musical, video and other audio material of educational value. The Internet also enables researchers and students to communicate directly with others with similar interests around the world. For this reason the Internet has been an extremely important resource for a large number of educational organisations for over a decade and the use of on-line services is well-established in the university and research environments. In recent years, other sectors of education including schools have begun to utilise on-line technologies to extend the reach and effectiveness of teachers' work in terms of curriculum development, delivery of material and provision of professional support and development services. The

Internet also offers new possibilities for 'open learning' and learning by distance education. This has enormous potential to increase access to educational facilities for those in rural or non-metropolitan communities. It also enables students to enrol in a course of study with educational institutions around the globe.

The Internet has the potential to become an important source of entertainment for users world wide. Already vast numbers of computer games, on-line magazines, newspapers, video and audio services are available on the Internet. Whilst many users can entertain themselves for hours 'surfing the net' for information, images and discussions regarding matters of interest to them, it is also important to note that in recent times many existing content industries are starting to use the Internet to deliver traditional audio and video products.

Although the bandwidth available in most countries currently precludes television broadcasts from easily being provided on-line, many predict that it is only a matter of time before full motion videos become widely available on the Internet. Over the next few years it is anticipated that the Internet will increasingly become a major source of the type of entertainment products which are currently available on television, radio, video and CD-ROM. As more secure methods of collecting payment for services over the Internet become available, it is expected that the Internet will also provide a common medium by which entertainment products are purchased.

The international, interactive and decentralised nature of the Internet and its potential for making available vast quantities of content to and from anywhere in the world give rise to a number of legal and ethical challenges. The following is not intended to be a complete discussion of all the issues which arise from the Internet, but an outline of some of those issues which create significant challenges, particularly in relation to content.

Any individual who has access to the Internet can participate in the many modes of communication which function in the on-line environment, expressing their views in the form of text, images, or sound and accessing the vast array of content provided by others. For this reason the Internet has enormous potential to create a dynamic international on-line community in which the relative parity amongst users enhances freedom of speech and cultural, social, political, religious and linguistic diversity.

However, it is important to recognise the critical role which access and active participation will play in this equation. Equitable access to the Internet remains a fundamental issue which will impact on the ability of individuals to participate in the benefits available through the Internet. This will be affected by the economic paradigms operating within both national and household frameworks.

The nature of the available telecommunications infrastructure and the costs of connecting to the network, typically via a service provider, will also impact on the opportunities presented to any given individual. Accordingly, ensuring equity of access to on-line services is emerging as a major challenge which is likely to have a concomitant impact on the issue of access to information, educational facilities and cultural resources and all of the opportunities which flow from these. It is also recognised that whilst the Internet provides the opportunity for immense diversity of content, at least at present, a significant proportion of Internet content appears to originate in Western liberal democracies, and particularly the United States. This material inevitably reflects some of the social, political and ethical values of those communities. A substantial proportion of Internet content is also only available in the English language. One of the challenges if the Internet is to reach its potential as a diverse medium will be to ensure that it does not become an increasingly homogenised environment which enhances the dominance of particular languages and cultural perspectives. In this regard it is noted that many countries have adopted strategies for television and radio to ensure local content and community participation in those mediums. These strategies are not easily adopted or even appropriate for Internet communications.

To maximise the diverse content and range of cultural and linguistic perspectives which can be accessed on-line it will be important to not only maximise access to the Internet but also to encourage all participants in the on-line environment to play an interactive role and contribute to the body of data which can be accessed by others through that medium. If content is provided from a wide variety of sources then the Internet may can maximise its enormous potential as a source of cultural, political, ethical and linguistic diversity which can increase understanding of cross-cultural issues and perceptions. As many new and existing entertainment services, including video services, are delivered on-line in a manner which requires a more passive response from Internet users, it will be increasingly important to ensure that the Internet remains an interactive and participatory experience rather than become a predominantly passive medium.

Most countries in the world place some restrictions on the type of material which may be possessed and/or disseminated within their borders. The extent and degree to which material in any given country is subject to restrictions reflects its particular political, cultural, religious and legal traditions. These traditions vary immensely around the world. For example, in many countries it is an offence to disseminate certain types of explicitly sexual or extremely violent material. Some countries also make it an offence to publish and/or transmit material which vilifies on the basis of gender, race or sexual orientation. In other countries it is an offence to publish material which criticises the government or may threaten national or racial harmony. In most countries certain dealings concerning child pornography are prohibited. However, the features of the on-line environment, including the vast amount of content which is available on the Internet, the international source of much of that content and the fact that the Internet is decentralised, make it extremely difficult to prevent material which contravenes the laws of any particular country from being provided or accessed across national boundaries. The inconsistency between the laws of different countries means that material which may be illegal in one country may be stored and subsequently accessed from countries where the material is legal. It may also be transmitted through a number of other countries, each of which has its own laws regarding the material.

Even where there is some consistency across jurisdictions relating to certain material, such as child pornography, the specific provisions of the various laws relating to the topic can differ significantly, making prosecution and international cooperation difficult. Even determining what is illegal in any particular country can be difficult due to the generality of the various national laws. For example, laws often set out broad categories of restricted material, such as 'obscene' material, and rely on the discretion of courts to give content to the prohibition. This makes it particularly difficult to identify what is prohibited in any given country at any given time. The ability to communicate anonymously in the on-line environment, which enables users to express themselves in a manner that may not be possible in the off-line world, also renders detection of those providing and accessing material which is prohibited extremely difficult. Anonymous re-mailing services can exacerbate this difficulty as Internet messages can be re-routed and copied in such a way that it is not possible to reliably ascertain their source. The encryption of content adds a further dimension to the difficulties of dealing with illegal material in the on-line environment.

Whilst certain kinds of content may be appropriate for adults to access, it may be unsuitable for children. Material which is sexually explicit or violent is often included in the type of content which is considered unsuitable or harmful for minors. Perceptions about the types of material which are suitable for children and young people vary immensely not only across national boundaries but also across cultures, religions and political systems. In some communities there is a high level of concern regarding sex and nudity, while in others material containing violent matter or drug abuse is considered to be the most offensive. Even within fairly homogeneous cultures there may be a wide range of differing views held about the appropriateness of certain material for minors, particularly where the material relates to sex, nudity, violence, language, and drug use. In existing media many mechanisms have been adopted to minimise children's access to unsuitable material.

These range from age restrictions on material which can be purchased or screened in cinemas to time zone classifications which restrict the type of programs which can be screened on television at times when children are likely to be watching. However, the availability of material which is considered unsuitable or harmful for minors presents particular challenges in the context of the Internet.

The Internet allows material to be accessed at any time in an interactive manner. Most material is not restricted in any way, the main exception being material which requires credit card details or some other form of payment is required. Accordingly, there is growing concern about the ability of minors to access material which is unsuitable for them but at the same time a recognition of the rights of adults to provide and access material which is legal in the off-line world. In response to this concern a number of technical options, including filter software products and the Platform for Internet Content Selection (PICS) have been developed. One of the important challenges in this area will be to ensure that these products are able to accommodate the diverse range of views and cultural perspectives which prevail around the world in relation to the protection of minors.

The international and decentralised nature of the Internet gives rise to a vast range of issues which challenge the mechanism previously used to deal with these matters on a domestic basis. The issues raised in the on-line environment include privacy, intellectual property, defamation, issues of electronic commerce and consumer protection, taxation and on-line gambling, along with illegal content and content which may be harmful to minors, to name a few. The role and responsibilities which service providers can and should have in relation to these matters is an area in respect of which there has been widespread debate and raises many technical, legal and philosophical issues. Part of the difficulty stems from the complex nature of the service providers role in relation to providing, disseminating and enabling access to content.

In some situations service providers seek to exercise some control over the content that is available through their service whilst in others they may have no knowledge or ability to control the content which is provided or accessed by users or content providers. In such an environment it is extremely difficult to allocate legal responsibility in same the manner that may have been possible in traditional broadcasting and publication models, creating many legal and ethical uncertainties.

The Internet presents immense legal and ethical challenges, particularly in relation to content. It must be accepted that by its very nature the Internet cannot be controlled by any central body and that its dynamic nature means that it is impossible to even assess the amount or nature of Internet content at any given time.

However, many argue that does not mean that nothing can or should be done about content on the Internet. There have been a number of regulatory responses adopted or proposed in several parts of the world which seek to address some of the issues relating to on-line content. These regulatory responses include:

1. the development of codes of practice for service providers with varying degrees of governmental input;
2. the application of existing legislation or the introduction of specific legislation penalising dealings

with certain on-line content, along with the establishing of e-mail hotlines for the reporting of 'illegal' content;

3. technical developments for controlling children's access to Internet content, including filter software and content labelling; and

4, the adoption of programs for community education.

A number of international bodies have also begun to consider the issues raised by the growth of the Internet, and the opportunities for international cooperation.

Codes of practice, or codes of conduct as they are sometimes called, are increasingly being used in various industries around the world to provide a regulatory framework which is more flexible than legislàtion and in respect of which the relevant industry plays an important role. Codes of practice may be developed entirely by industry, or they may be developed following a consultative process between industry and government. In some cases codes of practice operate within class licensing regimes. Codes of practice, mainly for service providers, are being developed in a number of different countries to try and address some of the issues arising in the on-line environment by setting out goals and best practices for participants in the on-line environment. The codes may deal with a wide range of issues, including but not limited to the rights and responsibilities of relevant parties in regard to providing and accessing content, the minimum age of subscribers, privacy and data protection, fair trading, advertising and promotional material, and the provision of information about the options available to parents to manage children's access to material which may be unsuitable to them.

In Australia a substantially self-regulatory regime for on-line services was recommended by the Australian Broadcasting Authority in its Investigation into the Content of On-Line Services: Report to the Minister for Communications and the Arts, delivered in June 1996 . The report recommended that industry codes of practice should be developed by on-line service providers. The main elements of the proposed regulatory framework are:

1. the identification of matters which should be included in codes of practice for service providers, which provide appropriate community safeguards, including complaints handling procedures;
2. the registration by the ABA of such codes of practice, developed by service providers after a process of public consultation; and
3. the monitoring of the codes of practice, and their effectiveness, by the ABA.

The matters identified for inclusion in the codes include age verification procedures which aim to limit the holding of open on-line accounts to persons over the age of 18 years; the adoption of procedures to deal with illegal material; the provision of information for users and content providers on legislation which may be relevant in an on-line environment; and the provision of information to users regarding filter products or on-line services which are available to those who wish to restrict access to material which may be unsuitable for children. It was also proposed that the codes should encourage content providers to label their content in accordance with PICS compatible labels. In the United Kingdom the on-line industry has developed a self-regulatory regime which has the support of the Department of Trade and Industry, the Metropolitan Police and the Home Office.

The central tenet of the scheme is the Safety-Net initiative which has the support of the Internet Service Providers Association (ISPA), along with the London Internet Exchange (LINX).

The scheme involves three key elements; rating content; reporting of content which may be illegal; and the exercise of responsibility by service providers in putting in place appropriate procedures to deal with illegal material once it has been identified. As part of the scheme ISPA has developed a draft code of practice as a starting point from which a more comprehensive code could be developed. The current draft code requires ISPA members to use their reasonable endeavours to ensure that services and promotional material does not contain content which is in breach of the law; encourages anything which is in any way illegal; contains material which incites violence, sadism, cruelty or racial hatred; or facilitates prostitution. The code also addresses matters of data protection, fair trading, pricing information and complaints procedures. The UK Government has stated that service providers who cooperate with the Safety-Net proposals will reduce their risk of prosecution by demonstrating that they have done all that can reasonably be expected to comply with the law.

A somewhat different regulatory scheme has emerged in Singapore. In that country a class licensing scheme for the Internet has been developed . Under the scheme Internet service providers must register with the Singapore Broadcasting Authority (SBA) and comply with the conditions of the class license. All licensed Internet service providers and relevant Internet Content providers are required to comply with the Internet Content Guidelines which have been developed as part of the scheme and satisfy the SBA that they have taken adequate steps to fulfil this requirement. Service providers must also develop Acceptable Use Policies for Internet account holders and comply with any codes of practice as the SBA issues from time to time. In Malaysia, a major source of regulation to date has been the conditions of service pertaining to the state owned Joint Advanced Research Integrated Networking (JARING) network. These set out the rules applying to Internet services and include the provisions that those using the network shall not use it for any activities not allowed under any law of Malaysia . Until recently the JARING was the only service provider in Malaysia but recently a second operator, Malaysia Telekom Berhad, is reported to have begun trading in Malaysia.

Most countries have some laws which makes it an offence to publish and/or distribute certain material. In some countries it is also an offence to possess certain material, such as child pornography. In some cases existing legislation regarding the publication, distribution and possession of certain types of content has been drafted in a manner which enables it to encompass material transmitted and accessed on-line. However, in other jurisdictions specific legislation to deal with illegal content in the on-line environment has been proposed or introduced.

In Singapore licensees are required to use their best efforts to ensure that their services does not include Internet content which is 'against the public interest, public order, national harmony or which offends against good taste or decency'. The scheme identifies particular Internet content which falls within this category. This includes, inter alia, content "which propagate permissiveness or promiscuity", "tends to bring the Government of Singapore into hatred or contempt, or which excites disaffection against the Government of Singapore." In contrast it seems that at least some content of this nature would not be illegal in the United Kingdom and Australia.

In the United Kingdom codes of practice are being utilised to place obligations on service providers to deal with, and where possible, remove illegal content from their servers once it has been identified. In exchange for complying with these procedures service providers may receive some protection from prosecution . In Australia the proposed regulatory regime also envisages that codes of practice for service providers will include appropriate procedures to deal with illegal content if and when it has been brought to a service providers attention. It has been suggested that compliance with codes of practice could be a defence in any prosecution against a service provider.

One of the recent responses to the issue of illegal content has been the setting up of reporting agencies, often referred to as 'e-mail hotlines'. These agencies enable Internet users who locate content which they believe is illegal to report their finding to a reporting agency which will investigate the content and may take action in relation to the material. To date e-mail hotline services have been identified in Singapore and the United Kingdom. In the United Kingdom an e-mail hotline has been set up under the Safety-Net Initiative. The Hotline service is operated by Internet Watch and "aims to enhance the enormous potential of the Internet to inform, educate, entertain and conduct business by ... hindering the use of the Internet to transmit material which is illegal in the UK". The first priority of the scheme is child pornography.

Internet Watch operates by encouraging Internet users to report content which they believe to be child pornography. Reports can be made by telephone, facsimile or e-mail and should contain a brief description of the material in question and the location of the site (i.e the world wide web address or the Usenet newsgroup details).

Upon receiving a report Internet Watch examines the material and if it considers it illegal will seek to trace its origins. Where the material has been identified as being sourced within the United Kingdom then Internet Watch will request that the relevant service provider contact the person who has placed the material on-line and seek to have the material removed. If material is not removed and/or if it involves child pornography, then Internet Watch will forward details to the Police. Under the scheme the police are to provide feedback to Internet Watch on the outcome of their report. Where the material is sourced from outside of the United Kingdom then Internet Watch will forward to the police the information about the site who will notify the relevant overseas law enforcement agency.

In Singapore, as part of its regulatory regime established in July 1996, the Singapore Broadcasting Authority has also set up a 'hotline' for identifying 'objectionable content'. The SBA has stated that the success of Internet content will depend very much on industry self-regulation and community action and has welcomed public assistance in the identification of material which is considered 'objectionable' under the laws of Singapore. Reports can be made by e-mail, telephone or post. In Australia the Australian Broadcasting Authority in its Report on the Content of On-Line Services supported in principle the establishment of e-mail hotlines for the reporting of child pornography. The ABA understands that the police bodies and law enforcement bodies are presently examining the viability of establishing such an agency in Australia.

Parental or teacher supervision is the most effective way of managing children's access to the Internet. However, it is widely recognised that this is not always possible and over the last decade, a range of software products have been developed for use on computers in the home and in schools in response to the perceived need for parents, teachers and supervisors to filter out or block Internet content which they do not consider suitable for minors in their care. Filter software can be provided to the user by the on-line service provider or purchased independently by the consumer for use at the individual computer level.

Some service providers also offer a filtering service which is specifically designed for use by minors. Filtering programs work in three main ways:

1. sites are blocked with reference to a list of known newsgroups, world wide web sites, File Transfer Protocol (FTP) and Gopher sites. Censoring decisions may be made centrally by the software producer with sites updated regularly, and/or by users instructing their system to block a particular site(s);

2. requests for, or receipt of, information which contains specified keywords or phrases are blocked. The keywords or phrases can be specified by the software manufacturer or by the end users who can manage the blocking of web sites by entering keywords and phrases in accordance with criteria they consider appropriate; and

3. all sites are blocked except those which are specified by the supervisor ('blanket blocking'). These programs usually provide an original unblocked list of known educational sites, and the supervisor is able to unblock new sites through a password secured interface.

Some products enable parents to combine some of these functions, while others offer additional features such as auditing of all on-line activity, including listing sites accessed, restricting the amount of time spent on-line and limiting access to some services such as bulletin boards. Whilst the first generation of filter products offer parents some tools to control their children's access to unsuitable material, some users have found that they have a number of limitations. For example, products which are based on recognition of keywords and phrases are not able to filter explicit graphic images or deal with encrypted data or transposed text. Conversely, sites of value to the user may also be blocked if they contain specified keywords or phrases. For example, press reports stated that at one time access to the White House web site was blocked by a filter responding to the word 'couple'. Where software producers are responsible for the blocking of material they may restrict content which is considered acceptable to the parent/supervisor. Where filter software operates by means of 'blanket' blocking, access to a considerable amount of potentially valuable material would be denied and parents and teachers would in many cases have to allocate considerable resources to enable access to appropriate material. However, there have been some recent international developments with content and selection software which have provided additional options for parents. This technology is called the Platform for Internet Content Selection (PICS). PICS was developed by the World Wide Web Consortium (W3C). W3C is a non-governmental cross-industry group which has offices in USA, France and Japan and comprises representatives of the computer, communications and content industries, as well as trade associations and public interest groups. PICS works by establishing a series of file formats that allows independent rating services to label Internet content in a form that can be recognised by PICS enabled software. The PICS labelling conventions do not dictate the use of any particular labelling scheme or determine who should pay attention to which labels.

The PICS technology allows any organisation or individual to develop a labelling system which reflects their tastes and standards and, if they wish, enable others to also use these labels. PICS compatible software can be set to block out all unrated content, or to only block content which has been rated in a certain manner. There are a number of scenarios in which PICS labels can be used. For example, labels may be developed to indicate whether Internet content contains sexual or violent material, enabling parents to select or block the material accordingly. A teacher might label a set of materials which are relevant to an astronomy lesson and block student access to everything else during that class. Those concerned about Nazi propaganda and other hate-speech available on-line, could label material that is historically inaccurate or that promotes hate, and businesses may wish to use labels to block their employees from visiting recreational sites during hours of office hours. Labelling can be applied directly by content providers at the time or after a site is posted on the Internet or it can be applied by a third party in accordance with an established labelling system. The creators of PICS envisaged that it could be used to support a large number of different labelling schemes which may have a multitude of different purposes. A number of organisations have already begun to establish labelling schemes which can interact with the PICS standards, most of which have been developed in North America and aim to assist parents in managing their children's access to Internet content. Examples are the Recreational Software Advisory Council labelling scheme for the Internet (RSACi), SafeSurf, Cyber Patrol and Net Shepherd.

One of the PICS compatible labelling schemes which has gained increasing prominence is the descriptive labelling scheme developed by the Recreational Software Advisory Council (RSAC) and is discussed below by way of example. The RSACi labelling system addresses four matters. These are the level of violence, sex, nudity, and language, including hate language, which a site contains. Internet content can be given a rating between 0 and 4 on each of these topics. The label aims to provide a description of the content in an Internet site rather than make a judgement about the appropriateness of content for any given audience or purpose. In some ways the descriptive RSAC labels can be seen as analogous to the labels applied to foodstuffs which merely provide information about ingredients of a product, rather than vouch for its suitability for consumption. One of the uses of a descriptive labelling schemes is that it enables parents to set their own standards about the material which they or their children access. For example, parents who are concerned about sexual content are able to set their PICS compatible software to block out material which has been given a high rating for sexual content. Other parents may be more concerned about language and/or violence and so can also can set their software to block out highly rated material of this nature. If the material has been rated then parents can use the labels to control Internet content, regardless of where they or the content is located. Importantly, those who are not concerned to block their own access to Internet materials need not activate those tools.

A proliferation of PICS compatible labelling schemes, perhaps being developed by a range of industry, community and governmental bodies around the world could serve many functions, including giving consumers a range of choices in relation to the values and perspectives which underpin the various labelling schemes and the purposes for which they can be used. This has the ability to reflect a diversity of different cultures and values and provide individuals with real choices about the filtering software and nature of Internet content which they access. However, for labels to be a truly effective tool for parents and supervisors many argue that a critical mass of content needs to be labelled. This raises the issue of whether it would be advantageous to develop a small number of international labelling schemes which can be widely recognised by content providers and users around the globe.

The Safety-Net initiative developed in the United Kingdom originally supported the use of the RSACi labeling scheme and proposed that service providers require their users to rate their web sites using RSACi labels. However, the ABA understands that there have been some recent developments in this regard and that Internet Watch Foundation has undertaken to work with the on-line industry in that country to develop a PICS compatible labeling scheme which meets the specific requirements of users in the United Kingdom. In

Australia labelling Internet content was given detailed consideration in the ABA's Report into the Content of On-Line Services. While recognising that labelling schemes might have many uses, the protection of children from unsuitable material was seen as one of the primary uses. The Report recommended that an On-Line Labelling Task Force be established to encourage development of an Australian labelling scheme for on-line content which was compatible with PICS or any superior standards which might be developed. The ABA is also conscious of the need to ensure that an Australian Labelling scheme is, as far as possible, consistent with international ratings developments. This is to ensure that Australian content providers and users of the labelling schemes are not disadvantaged in terms of both having Australian content accessed by users around the world, or accessing a wide variety of material when using utilising the labels.

Under the Singaporean regulatory regime for on-line services, localized service providers and parents are encouraged to use filter software products such as Net Nanny, SurfWatch, Cyber Patrol and Net Shepherd. The ABA notes that some of these filter products are compatible with the PICS standards. As an additional measure to protect young Internet users the SBA also requires schools, libraries and Internet service providers which provide access to children to institute tighter levels of controls. The SBA has announced that it is presently working with the Minister of Education and National Library Board to identify options for implementing an acceptable level of control.

The potential benefits of the on-line environment for enhancing the way we communicate, educate, inform and entertain ourselves has been widely recognised.

However, it is also recognised that community understanding of the nature of on-line services, including the opportunities which they present and the options available for managing children's access to those services will be critical if the Internet is to be used in the most productive manner. Many countries have adopted or proposed strategies for enhance community understanding of the Internet and the opportunities which it offers. A priority for many of these programs is parental education, as many parents feel that they do not have as much experience in relation to on-line services as their children and therefore are unable to effectively utilise some of the technical options available to them for limiting children's access to unsuitable Internet content. A number of programs have also been proposed or introduced to enhance the knowledge and technical ability of teachers who will play an important role in ensuring that children are able to maximise the benefits of on-line services.

In Australia the importance of community education in terms of promoting the most beneficial use of the Internet and ensuring that users, particularly parents, were aware of the options available for managing children's access was recognised in the ABA's Report on its Investigation into On-line Services. The report recommended, inter alia, that a community education strategy be developed to provide information about on-line services and that the strategy target parents and guardians. It was proposed that information might be distributed via school and parent networks, at the point of sale for computer hardware and software, as well as on relevant web sites. The report also recommended that research be undertaken by the ABA and other relevant bodies to assist in determining the requirements of parents and guardians in relation to managing children's access to Internet content.

There have also been a number of initiatives developed in the school environment. These include the Education Network Australia (EdNA) project which obtained in principle agreement form all Australian, State and Territory Governments at a meeting of the Ministerial Council on Education, Employment, Training and Youth Affairs in May 1995. The project aims to provide Australia wide access to educational products and services relevant to Australian educators. Another project which has been developed is oz-TeacherNet.This is a service which has been developed to meet the needs of teachers to make greater use of the resources, professional development and curriculum opportunities which the Internet offers. In terms of student usage, a number of different approaches have been adopted by schools to manage access to unsuitable material, including the development of acceptable use policies, student contracts, and restricting access to particular sites or Internet functions such as newsgroups at the school or service provider level.

In Malaysia, as part of the drive to ensure the success of the Multimedia Super Corridor (MSC), a number of major initiatives are being undertaken. One of these is the connection of all schools within the MSC to the Internet by 1998. In a speech for the opening of Multimedia Asia on 1 August 1996, the Prime Minister of Malaysia, Yab Dato Seri Dr Mahathir Bin Mohamad announced that the Malaysian Government is working to increase the role of multimedia in education: Teachers will need to change their role in the electronic classroom from being information providers to counsellors in order to help the students know how to select information sources, to make judgements about what they are downloading ... The measure of our success in 2020 will be the number and quality of our people who can add value to information. To that end, we will be creating a Multimedia University and technology schools within the MSC.

In Singapore the SBA has expressed an intention to complement its regulatory regime with public education initiatives which alert parents to the ways in which they may protect their children from 'objectionable material and cyberspace abuses'. As part of its strategy the SBA has also set up a web site called 'Tips for Parents' page. In the UK there have been a number of initiatives undertaken by various organisations which seek, amongst other things, to enhance community understanding of the Internet and provide some guidance for parents on how they might manage their children's use of the Internet. NCH Action for Children, Britain's largest child care charity, provides an example of a non-government organisation (NGO) on-line initiative aimed at educating parents about the Internet. The organisation's web site includes a 'Parent's Guide to the Internet' and advice on getting the best from the Internet. It also attempts to explain some commonly used Internet jargon, as well as provides some useful contacts. These contacts include the NETCOM parent's advice line, a 24 hour telephone advice line, and the parents information network. The network is a national information technology organisation offering help to parents who want to use computers with their children. The 'Useful Contacts' page also includes hyperlinks to the PICS and RSACi web sites. In July 1996 the House of Lords Select Committee on Science and Technology published a report titled Information Society: Agenda for Action in the UK on 23 July 1996. The report contained 40 recommendations for action to promote the development of the Information Society. A number dealt with information technology in schools and the Government has responded to the Report with a number of strategies to improve teacher competence in this area and increase the number of schools connected to the Internet.

There has been an increasingly amount of discussion regarding the importance of international cooperation in maximising the opportunities and meeting some of the challenges presented by the Internet. Two international bodies who have recently focussed on these issues are the European Commission (EC) and Organisation for Economic Cooperation and Development (OECD). The European Commission (EC), in its Green Paper on the Protection of Minors and Human Dignity in Audiovisual and Information Services, considered that the main tasks which the on-line industry should address are:

1. drawing up a code of conduct and concrete measures within a framework defined by cooperation between national government departments;
2. identifying areas where there may be a need for common standards on the labelling of material; and
3. promoting the PICS standard or equivalent systems with a view to reaching, as quickly as possible, a critical mass of labelled material, navigation systems and/or parental control devices which are mutually compatible.

The Report of the European Commission's Working Party on Illegal and Harmful Content on the Internet has also proposed, inter alia, that a self-regulatory scheme be developed for the on-line environment comprising:

1. a code of conduct for Internet service providers, including access providers, host service providers and anonymous re-mailers; ?a hot-line for complaints from the public, with appropriate safeguards against misuse; and
2. an independent self-regulatory body, including representatives of industry and users, to advise on whether or not a breach of the code of conduct has occurred (without prejudice to the due process of law).

The Organisation for Economic and Cultural Development (OECD) has recently been asked to consider two proposals concerning the regulation of the Internet. The first of these is a proposal of the French Government for a general agreement on international cooperation for regulation of the Internet with a view to enhancing the economic and cultural potential of the Internet and to combat illegal activities.

The proposal points to three priority areas for cooperation:

1. the definition of a typology of players and the methodological rules to be applied;
2. a list of guidelines aimed at guaranteeing the respect of basic ethical rules and improving consumer protection; and
3. principles for judicial and police cooperation.

Signatories to the agreement will promote the establishment by economic players of a voluntary code of conduct. The codes are to safeguard various principles, including the principle of respect for human dignity and of public order (in particular through use of filtering software), the principle of protection of privacy, and the principle of consumer protection. The Belgian government has also recently put forward a proposal to the OECD for a convention aimed at prohibiting the transmission on the Internet of content that encourages the exploitation of and sexual violence to children. The ABA understands that this matter is presently being considered by the Committee for Information, Computer and Communications Policy (ICCP).

The unique features of the Internet give rise to an environment which provides enormous opportunities for enhanced communication and civic participation, education and entertainment for individuals and organisations around the world. The Internet has the potential to reflect a diverse range of cultural, political, religious and linguistic perspectives and enhance our understanding of across different cultures. But along with these immense opportunities, the Internet also presents a number of particular challenges.

Privacy on Internet

The impacts of Globalization, Relativism, the New World Order, Materialism, Egocentricism, Hyper Consumerism, invasive technologies, the uncontrollable flood of information, the advent of genetic manipulation and perhaps genetic control, the corrosion of the notion of the sacred in modern post-industrial societies and many other factors have disturbed the ladder of values in each and every society. The insatiable greed for more instant pleasure has added a spinning potential to the tempo of change. Due to this uncontrollable hyper acceleration in all the venues of life including cyber crime, some would state that a rational utilitarian scale of values could govern human behaviour.

As mentioned in Sautter's report "To prevent the loss of hundreds of thousands of dollars in wasted man-hours and bandwidth more and more employers are using special software to monitor their employees' Web browsing and e-mail traffic". Marketers can spy on you by using cookies. A cookie is a unique text file that is placed on your hard drive the first time you access certain websites. It is like a personal serial number used to identify your computer on your next visit to the site but the cookie also enables the marketers to gather information about your browsing preferences.

According to the Washington based privacy research group EPIC, 86 out of 100 tested online companies work with cookies. The gathered information about the customers could be sold to other persons or entities".Hackers can spy on you by using Trojan horses coming in the guise of backdoor computer programs which once infiltrating into your computer allows hackers to access it and take control. Hackers can even spy on your E-mail as it passes through the several web servers. At any of these relay points your message is vulnerable to snooping.

Skillful hackers can also hijack a router and then read or mess around with the text messages stored in it. Sniffer programs may scan traffic for specified terms, cyber snoops can capture Internet account login IDS & passwords and use them to surf the web at owner's expense and web based E-mail services are particularly open to intruders. Some sovereign states run electronic surveillance systems around the world and scan the web for signs of criminal activity, monitoring E-mail communications eavesdropping on chat room conversations and generally tracking the traffic on the net. Echelon, a massive cold war-era surveillance network run by the intelligence services of the U.S., U.K., Canada New Zealand and Australia, is the world's most extensive spy system for nonmilitary targets and the one most likely to be watching as you roam the Web. Some 90% of Net traffic is said to be scanned by Echelon. Several countries also run their own national Web surveillance systems.

According to Duncan Campbell "the Echelon system can access and process all of the world's satellite communications automatically". A large part of Echelon is devoted to the INTELSAT network of Geo stationary communications satellites. Cable tapping is harder, however, as with cryptography itself Echelon is fighting a loosing battle.

As more and more phones become low power digital devices, the range over which they can be monitored and the effort needed to decode them increases, a brand new wireless technology called pulse wireless - already used by the security services - promises to make many transmission virtually undetectable. By autumn of this year, the Echelon interception system will be subject to a legal battle that threatens to blow the lid on this covert surveillance network Echelon when the issue reaches the courts.

David Nataf of the Jean Pierre Millet law firm in Paris is leading the assault on America's National Security Agency (NSA). The plaintiffs, several French corporations and individuals who cannot be identified, allege that the (NSA) has spied on them illegally. He says his team has enough evidence against the (NSA) to pursue damages for lost business and for illegal covert activity. At the center of the allegations is evidence implicating the (NSA's) involvement in spying on European nations' commercial dealings. Nataf's team will try to convince the American courts that stolen information was passed onto US companies, giving them an unfair advantage over their French competitors.

In March 2000, a former CIA director, James Woolsey, confirmed that the US monitors European communications to keep an eye on any economic bribery activities. "We have spied on that (bribery) in the past," said Woolsey responding to the (Interception Capabilities 2000) report presented to the parliament's Citizens Rights Committee. "I hope that the United States government continues to spy on bribery". The controversial impact of Echelon was also apparent on a broader platform, in July 2000 the European Parliament voted to set up a Temporary Committee of inquiry on the Echelon interception system.

It is suggested that multinational companies may have taken their cue from Echelon and are carrying out their own surveillance work. Some have suggested they may even cooperate with secret government snooping. Industrial espionage is not a new phenomenon, but as information becomes ever more vital to companies and integral to their practices it is easy to see that the incentives are greater than ever.

A Scientific and Technical Options Assessment (STOA) report called Development of Surveillance Technology and Risk of Abuse of Economic Information presented to the European Union December 1999 concludes that: "Although it is very difficult to quantify the losses caused by industrial espionage, the losses incurred by European firms can reasonably be put at several billion Euros per year". These are some of the issues affecting the Right of Privacy on the networks. The matrix of interceptors includes individuals, corporations, multinational companies and even sovereign states. Efforts are evolving to inquire into these interception activities and even to condone their acts pursuant to the right of privacy on the networks and global communication. As with any issue involving communities at large, a multitude of interception techniques have been described and elaborated on. Some even sound extremely credible and others are generally discarded as unimaginable at the current state of technology.

Legal Protection to Privacy

The law has a functional role by deterring any potential perpetrator from committing a criminal act and it also has a curative effect in devolving compensations for damages if an illicit act is committed. The legal texts covering this area are various as we have previously mentioned and they constitute two faces of one coin. One face is information protection laws and the other is telecommunications protection laws. Their symbiotic effect produces the legal deterrent and protection. To be criminalized and penalized by the law, the acts of violation of the right of privacy should constitute crimes in conformity with the old Latin rule. We should bear in mind that criminal law texts are interpreted very strictly.

In the modern world, we first find on the international level the international agreements and conventions such as:

I The Universal Declaration of Human Rights in which Article 12 states that: "No one shall be subjected to arbitrary interference with his privacy, or correspondence, Everyone has the right to the protection of the law against such interference". A key word in this Article is (arbitrary). Lawful interference is not excluded.

II The International Covenant on Civil and Political Rights. This UN Covenant builds on the Universal Declaration and is legally binding.

By Art. 2.1, the Contracting Parties are obliged to respect and ensure all of the rights recognized by the Covenant, and by Art. 2.2 they are required to take steps to meet their obligations within their own legal systems. Art. 4 allows Contracting Parties to derogate from some of the specific Articles (i.e. Rights) in a Public Emergency. Article 17 states that: "No one shall be subjected to arbitrary or unlawful interference with his privacy" and that: "Everyone has a right to the protection of the law against such interference". This appears to address only natural, not legal persons and reinforces the idea that lawful interference is permitted". The second layer of legal sources comprises the national legislations either enacted by parliament in the form of legislations and acts or in some countries by means of presidential decrees and in said context, we state the situation of the legislation in some developed countries.

In the U.S.A., privacy on the networks is protected by "the Federal Electronic Communications Act (ECPA), which protects all forms of electronic communications - telephone voice communications as well as computer digital communication. ECPA applies to the government as well as private persons and entities. It prohibits any person from intentionally, intercepting an electronic communication, or from disclosing the contents of any intercepted electronic communication unlawfully. It applies not only to hackers but also to those who own and operate such systems such as an internet access provider, a private network operator, the sys-op of a computer bulletin board and the like.

ECPA also prohibits any person or entity who provides an electronic communication service to the public from divulging the contents of any communication. The anonymity of communications emanates according to the U.S. Supreme Court from the right to speak anonymously and is protected by the first amendment to the US constitution. ECPA in the USA sets in place a procedure to authorize lawful interception. Network operators and service providers are required by CALEA (the Communication Assistance for Law Enforcement Act) to have the necessary technical facility and to render assistance to law enforcement agencies. The Foreign Intelligence Surveillance Act of 1978 (FISA) authorized electronic surveillance of foreign powers and agents of foreign powers is regulated to protect the US national security.

To target communications need not relate to any crime, FISA surveillance action are implemented operationally by FBI. Said surveillance is classified. In addition to said legal vehicles the Privacy Act of 1974 imposes limits on the collection and use of personal information by federal government agencies. The Privacy Protection Act of 1980 establishes safeguards relating to materials held by a person reasonably believed to have a purpose to publish a newspaper, book, broadcast, or similar public communication.

The Fair Credit Reporting Act of 1970 regulates information maintained by creditors. The Right to Financial Privacy Act restricts government access to the financial report of any financial institutional customer. The Telephone Consumer Protection Act of 1991 protects the consumer from advertising via e-mail. In addition to a plethora of state laws and regulations. However, the situation in the European Union is thoroughly exposed as can be seen in the comprehensive study prepared by Dr. Chris Elliot for the scientific and technological option assessment program of the European Parliament. According to the executive summary of said precious study "the EU countries are committed by international treaties, EU decisions and directives and each national country by its national laws. Most countries have legal recognition of the right of privacy of personal data and many require telecommunications network operators to protect the privacy of their users.

All EU countries permit the use of encryption for data transmitted via public telecommunications networks (except France where this will shortly be permitted). Electronic commerce requires secure and trusted communications and may not be able to benefit from privacy law designed only to protect natural persons. The legal regimes reflect a balance between three interests: privacy; law enforcement; electronic commerce. Legal processes are emerging to satisfy the second and third interests by granting more power to governments to authorize interception (under legal controls) and allowing strong encryption with secret keys. There do not appear to be adequate legal processes to protect privacy against unlawful interception, either by foreign governments or by non-governmental bodies. A course of action open to the EU is to require telecommunications operators to take greater precautions to protect their users against unlawful interception. This would appear to be possible without compromising law enforcement or electronic commerce"

In Egypt, the right of privacy is governed in by consecutive layers of legal texts both on the supranational and the national levels. On the international level, Article 12 of The Universal Declaration Of Human Rights together with The International Covenants On The Civil And Political Rights are enforced according to Article 151 Para 1 of the Egyptian Constitution which stipulates the following: "The President of the republic shall conclude treaties and communicate them to the People's Assembly, accompanied with a suitable clarification. They shall have the force of law after their conclusion, ratification, and publication according to the established procedure". On the constitutional level, article 45 of the Egyptian Constitution stipulates the following: "The law shall protect the inviolability of the private life of citizens. Correspondence, wires, telephone calls and other means of communication shall have their own sanctity and secrecy and may not be confiscated, divulged or monitored, except by a causal judicial warrant and for a definite period according to the provisions of the law".

In the same context, Article 57 of the Constitution stipulates: "Any assault on individual freedom or on the inviolability of private life of citizens and any other public rights and liberties guaranteed by the Constitution and the law shall be considered a crime, whose criminal and civil lawsuit is not liable to prescription. The State shall grant a fair compensation to the victim of such an assault". We would like to state also that before the prevailing Constitution of 1971 the previous

Constitutions including the Constitution of 1923 safeguarded the right of privacy by stipulating in Article 11 "It is prohibited to divulge the secrets contained in letters, telegrams, phone communication except in the cases provided for in the law".On the legislative level, secrecy and privacy are maintained in several legislations such as Tax Laws, Banking Secrecy Law, The Laws pertaining to Correspondence and mail the laws pertaining to the Civil Status, the laws governing Statistics and Census, the Code of Criminal Procedures, the Penal Code and the Civil Code.

From the analysis of the texts of the constitution and the several legislations previously mentioned, we can conclude the following:

a) The right of privacy pertaining to personal data and information is protected both by constitutional texts and by legislative texts.

b) Eavesdropping, hacking, and unlawful surveillance by using phone lines as a medium of communication are penalized by the texts of the penal code. In the opinion of the majority of the Egyptian jurisprudence.

c) Privacy on the networks is in general protected by the texts of the prevailing laws.

d) To ensure maximum protection, amendments should be made to the text of Article 309 of the Egyptian Penal Code. To penalize eavesdropping, unlawful intrusion, or penetration or unlawful surveillance of telecommunications since the prevailing law protects phone conversations and the penal law is interpreted in the strict sense.

e) A new law governing telecommunications is on its

way to being discussed by the new parliament to be elected, this law organizes telecommunication. In said draft of law an article governing the secrecy of telecommunication is appearing. We shall see the final product after its enactment by the competent constitutional authorities.

f) Contractual undertakings to safeguard privacy may be added to any contracts.

Further elaboration leads me to display that the current Egyptian Civil Law distinctly provides for the right to demand for compensation sustained independently from the right of the state to impose penalties. Egyptian Civil Law stipulates in Article 50 the following:

> "A person whose rights inherent in his personality have been unlawfully infringed, shall have the right to demand the cessation of the infringement and compensation for any damage sustained thereby". And it stipulates in Article 163 the following: "Every fault which causes injury to another, imposes an obligation to make reparation upon the person by whom it is committed".

The sanctity of the right of privacy is protected by the civil law. If the right of privacy has been unlawfully infringed, the victim of said infringement shall have the right to demand before a court of law the cessation of infringement and compensation for any damage sustained thereby. The right to receive the compensation for damages according to the civil law is an independent right from the right of the state to impose corporal or financial penalties on the perpetrator of a crime committed in violation to the Right of Privacy and as mentioned previously. The perpetrator is penalized if proven guilty by imprisonment and/or fine.

The modern world is composed of independent sovereign states. Each sovereign state has its own constitution, laws, and competent courts. As a result of said situation, each law in each sovereign state determines the material acts that constitute a crime. As state laws differ in general from country to country, we are sometimes faced with the quandary of conflicting laws. Some examples can be as follows:Networks intrusion could be considered as a criminal act in a state and not considered as such in another state.A sovereign state may have a law penalizing the hacking and interception of messages on the networks and another state may not have in its legislations any text penalizing said act.

An individual may act innocently on the networks with a party in another sovereign state without real knowledge of the laws of the country with whom he is accessing through the networks and most probably said country would have a criminal text penalizing his behaviour and most probably another legal text stating that.

Furthermore, some procedural laws in several sovereign states would give to the public prosecution the right to prosecute specific crimes such as attempts to disrupt the national security of a state even if the act is perpetrated outside of the borders of said sovereign country. Accordingly, the conflict of laws is a crucial topic pertaining to the governance of the legal conduct on the networks.

The conflict of jurisdictions is another issue triggered by the fact that different Courts in different countries may be considered by each and every sovereign state as the competent courts to see into a case. The law of one country may indicate that a criminal court is competent to try an eavesdropping crime on the networks perpetrated by a citizen of a foreign country against an individual or an entity in the first country. On the other hand, the foreign country and according to its procedural laws may consider its courts competent since its citizen committed the crime on the soil of said country. A third country may consider its courts competent to view the same case before a state security court and not before a traditional criminal court since the act is considered according to said third country laws a state security crime. In one federal state, you may find conflict of laws and conflict of jurisdictions between state laws and federal laws, state courts and federal courts.

International treaties and conventions are the tools used in international law to homogenize the legal principles in the different sovereign states and to harmonize the stipulations of the different national laws & to solve the conflicts.

Due to the international aspect of most of the crimes perpetrated via the Internet or the other networks, the reasonable and ideal solution according to some lawyers would be the governance of the international networks by an international treaty containing positive clauses governing the behaviour of the individuals and entities on the networks and penalizing any infringement of the clauses of said treaty through international prosecution, courts and law enforcement agencies. Said idealistic approach should give rise to an international judiciary able and capable to issue orders and verdicts enforceable against the perpetrators of any criminal act on the net in the various jurisdictions. Said solution is a farfetched solution. A compromise could be reached by having an international treaty stating minimum requirements in the different national laws to safeguard the right of privacy and other rights on the net. In many countries including Egypt treaties and conventions when signed, approved, promulgated, and enacted by the parliament have the force of the national laws. The European model in this context is one of the successful models the model of the United States of America pertaining to the relation between the different states of the union and the supremacy of the federal laws. The elaboration by jurists and professionals of a model law to be used as an example by sovereign states to legislate internal laws, is also another solution. However, enforcement of the Law is a crucial issue facing several problems. In an attempt to display the current inherent difficulties faced in enforcement of the law:

1. The anonymity of the perpetrator;
2. The quasi immateriality of the criminal act that should be proven before a court of law according to procedural laws which are not always modeled to tackle cyber crime issues and especially the immateriality of the conduct on the networks and the immateriality of the evidence;
3. The technical incapability of most police forces to track and apprehend the perpetrator on line;
4. The geographical and territorial barriers; and
5. The preoccupation of the police force with other types of conventional crimes which are called natural crimes or with other life threatening crimes or national security issues and not with cyber crimes against natural personsÿ and many more aspects.

This enumeration is not a complete list but a count of the more relevant aspects that should be taken into consideration regarding enforcement of the law against perpetrators.

UNESCO Virtual Forum on INFOethics

VF-INFOethics is an open worldwide electronic discussion forum carried out from October 1997 to April 1998. This forum was organized as a follow-up to a recommendation made by the participants at the first INFOethics Congress held in Monaco from 10 to 12 March 1997. The forum was designed and managed by the Information Science Department of the University of Konstanz.

VF-INFOethics is not a substitute for meetings in a real-life environment — the advantage of face-to-face communication is too obvious and knowledge and experience with electronic forums is not yet wide-spread enough, at least not among UNESCO experts, who are normally not the typical Internet users. But experimenting with electronic forums can provide UNESCO with knowledge about the potentials of the new medium and can contribute to a more extended word-wide awareness about the importance of information ethics in a globalizing information society. VF-INFOethics thus supports UNESCO's objective as a world-wide laboratory of ideas, in this case via a forum on information ethics, identifying ethical principles, guiding action, devising immaterial strategies and mobilizing political leaders in their resolve to implement them. As potentials or value-added effects of electronic communication forums the following deserve mention:

- Electronic communication forums allow exchange of information between people who are not likely to meet in real life.
- Electronic communication forums, organized according to hypertext principles, allow flexible navigation in heterogeneous information material and can thus develop into a platform of knowledge with respect to the topic of the forum.
- Electronic communication forums, in a Web-based technical environment are normally organized in an asynchronous mode (although synchronous chat techniques or tele-conferencing facilities are becoming more and more available for forum purposes as well). Asynchronous communication allows quasi real-time reactions to the forum's statements but also allows delayed reactions after a period of information gathering or, simply, of thinking.
- Electronic communication forums, compared with the high costs for real conferences with participants from all over the world, are a cheap technology once the technical equipment is available.
- Electronic communication forums, in particular when data-base supported, allow flexible adaptation to different users' needs/expectations, or to users' dialogue behaviour, and to different pre-established parameters such as access and editing rights.

The hopes for VF-INFOethics were only moderately high because we could not expect that knowledge and experience with new electronic communication devices would be very advanced among UNESCO experts. This was all the more likely, given the fact that we tried to avoid an Anglo-saxon and Western-Europe dominated expertise and insisted instead on selecting people from all over the world. The particants were chosen on the basis of UNESCO expertise and recommendations from active members. Only these experts, altogether about 60, had the right to write, but the forum, as a WWW application, was open to the public for reading purposes. The forum's main objective was to augment knowledge and public awareness on topics concerning information ethics and to provide UNESCO with recommendations for further action in the field of information ethics based on the world-wide electronic discussion among experts in the field. In addition to statements from experts, additional information, for example references to pertinent literature on information ethics, to other web sites, to data bases, and to other discussion groups with a similar scope was provided by the central Constance monitoring group of VF-INFOethics. Additional links could be provided by all members of VF-INFOethics. VF-INFOethics has thus developed into an open forum, a platform, or a market place with numerous links to the world's knowledge on information ethics.

The INFOethics forum was carried out in two rounds. The first round lasted from October 97 until the end of the year 1998. The second round was opened for discussion as of Februar 20th 1998. At the end of round 2, UNESCO can be provided with recommendations for further action. It is very likely that the forum will continue to be an electronic floor for UNESCO-related discussions on INFOethics and will then be opened to a broader UNESCO public or to the public in general. This, of course, will raise many new problems. In the near future, the forum will be used before, during and after the second UNESCO conference on INFOethics, which will take place in October 1998, again in Monte Carlo. The software, which was developed for VF-INFOethics and which is continously being improved, can be used for other UNESCO activities, in particular by national commissions for UNESCO or for educational purposes. At the moment, we are using the VF-INFOethics software for a virtually organized course on information ethics in the information science curriculum at the University of Konstanz, Germany.

The forum was opened with a brief general statement about the concept of information ethics:

Information ethics, in general, is the study of commonly held values related to the belief in equality of access, justice and mutual respect arising from the development and application of new information and telecommunications technologies (e.g. the Internet).

Information ethics concerns many fields such as philosophy (ethics), anthropology/ethnology, linguistics, economics, law, sociology, political science, education, religion/theology, artificial intelligence, information and computer science. Information ethics covers both the private/individual and the public/institutional aspects of ethical problems, more and more on a global basis.

For many people, information ethics is likely to be considered as a substitute for traditional civic behavior in the advancing global information society. For UNESCO, information ethics is particularly related to science, education, culture, and civil society in general, both in developed and in developing countries.

The following questions were formulated with respect to the role of UNESCO on the topic ‚Information rich and information poor':

What can UNESCO do to prevent modern societies from being divided into the information elite and the information underprivileged? Is there a need and a chance for UNESCO to fill the widening "abstraction gap" between the dominant information rich and the information poor? Is UNESCO an appropriate advocate to defend the rights of the information underprivileged? What is the role of organizations such as UNESCO in overcoming the information and communication gap both within countries and between them?

With education being considered a major means to overcome the barriers between information rich and information poor - what can UNESCO do to help topics in information ethics be included in curricula at all levels of education?

Can UNESCO play a major role in programs designed to overcome the language barriers between people and nations? How can UNESCO protect the language rights of the non-English-speaking-world against economic interests in one-world-one-language markets?

When information competence is both the ability to access/use globally available information and the ability to produce information services - what can UNESCO do both to allow easy access to the global information resources and to move more passive (reading) societies into active (writing) societies?

What can UNESCO do to protect the rights of developing countries to represent their own way of thinking, of culture, science and economy in regional and global information networks and services?

The discussion on this topic was rather intensive. As a result of the discussion on the topic ,Information rich and information poor' the following recommendations were formulated.

- Bring net access to poor countries by putting existing resources to sensible use in order to promote the development of global and local information cultures and economies.
- Support the development of a World Information Ethos.
- Support concrete projects in information poor countries in order to create country-specific information centres.
- Public awareness on these matters through virtual forums, publications, and conferences should be promoted.
- Provide permanent, specific, and detailed knowledge of existing information activities in information poor countries.
- UNESCO should promote the rights of non-English-speaking-countries and their economic interests.
- UNESCO should promote topics in information ethics to be included in curricula at all levels.
- Promotion activities through international organizations should be based on grassroots efforts as well as on a decentralized and well coordinated basis.

The following questions were formulated with respect to the role of UNESCO on the topic Information as a public and/or a private good:

What can UNESCO do to help the development of public/private structures as an appropriate balance between economic and social interests? What can UNESCO do to achieve and finance the provision of information falling in the public domain to all members of the societies in all countries? What can UNESCO do to provide open access to the world public knowledge heritage? What can UNESCO do to develop a world-wide awareness for the importance of information and communication technologies and systems for all societies and for the balance between them?

As the result of the discussion on the topic ,Information as a public and/or private good' the following summary was formulated.

"Information as a public and/or a private good" stimulated some discussion about the status of information in modern societies. Some concern was expressed about the negative effects of modern information structures (virtualization) on the job market. The participants did not see any realistic alternative economic model by which the shortcomings of the neo-liberalism approach could be overcome. It was suggested that cooperatives may play a major role in the usage of information as a common good. UNESCO should not get involved in general abstract discussions about a new world order. Instead UNESCO should concentrate on feasible projects such as supporting efforts for the digitization of public information (as the world people's heritage) as a counterweight to the power of the market, where information is considered a commodity only.

The role of copyright should be reconsidered as well in order to define a new generally accepted fair use of information. By encouraging free access to the world's public knowledge (the people's own heritage) UNESCO can contribute to establishing a counterweight to the power of the market, where information is considered a commodity to be paid for. UNESCO should use a set amount of funds to support the digitization of public material (e.g. to finance portable scanners). The role of copyright (so far mainly used to enforce market rights) should be reconsidered. Particularly, the rights of users to access public materials should be balanced against the predominantly private exploitation of information. Preservation and transmission of information was considered as among the ethical responsibilities of the present for future generations.

The following questions were formulated with respect to the role of UNESCO on the topic, Trust, ownership, and validity of information in cyberspace':

What can be done by UNESCO in order to establish an ethics instrument for information/content providers by which they may be obliged to care for trustworthy, approved, or true information? Which is the main role of UNESCO in the new property right debate, for example on digital objects? What can UNESCO do to establish a new "fair use" and/or "copyleft" of information which establishes a compromise between the rights of the holders and the interests of society to have free access to information?

Can UNESCO play an active role in establishing trust in information services and electronic markets, in particular when sensitive subjects are involved, such as medicine, law, or political information? Is UNESCO an appropriate and world-wide accepted institution to develop, maintain, and survey generally accepted quality criteria for the reliability and authenticity of information services? What is the role of UNESCO in establishing trust in machine intelligence and services such as intelligent agents or in keeping it under public control?

There was an innovative and provocative proposal to rethink the role of copyright: It doesn't make any sense for authors who already get paid by public institutions to receive additional copyright income. Giving up copyright income could break the circle of high prices and lack of access, at least in scientific environments. Access to the world's knowledge should have higher priority than supporting commercial interest in information commodities. A different answer may be required with respect to entertainment and literature.

On the other hand it was not considered realistic that authors would voluntarily give up commercial rights. Therefore it is not sufficient to change our attitude towards ownership and profit. A solution could be for publishing companies to pay a certain percentage of the author's income to the public, which is explicitly designed for supporting the construction of a powerful and royalty-free world wide public domain of information. This idea of sharing profits from knowledge products can be extended to all organizations which produce value-adding information/knowledge products originally based on publicly produced and financed primary/raw information for the market.

UNESCO is not either WIPO or WTO (although the protection of authors/publishers' rights cannot be ignored, it is not the main concern for UNESCO). Instead UNESCO must bring its own added value to the debate on intellectual property rights, and this means to promote the free flow of ideas by word and image, to give fresh impulse to popular education, and to support all means for the diffusion of knowledge. All scientific articles produced by public universities or public laboratories could be made freely available on the servers of these institutions.

UNESCO should take the lead in a world wide movement to promote this public domain information, and present innovative ideas to ensure distribution and free access to it. In particular with respect to developing countries, economic barriers created by a purely market oriented approach towards knowledge and information need to be overcome. UNESCO should use all its prestige to convince governments and institutions involved in the information/knowledge industry all over the world that they should share profits from knowledge products (especially those which are originally based on publicly produced and financed primary/raw information) with public institutions. These institutions then can produce value-added free-access information for those who cannot afford to pay for it.

The following questions were formulated with respect to the role of UNESCO on the topic ,Privacy, confidentiality, security, hate, violence in the Internet':

What are appropriate measures for UNESCO in order to diminish the amount of violence and hate in the Internet? Is UNESCO the appropriate organization for developing a world-wide code for information privacy? Is such a code desirable or possible? What are appropriate control structures if such a privacy/confidentiality code were ever to be agreed on? What can UNESCO do to encourage and establish the free flow of information in the traditional and new media

Although the concept of information ethics was a topic of discussion in itself and was permanently referredto, there was no formal agreement about this concept besides general remarks such as that information ethics deals with principles of equality, justice and mutual respect under the conditions of a global information society.

Global networks and electronic market places and information services (in the Internet and other prorietary networks) are the environment and the only means in which and through which information ethics develops.

One can doubt whether there is a need (or a possibility) for something like information ethics (or science ethics or market ethics) in addition to ethics in general. The principles of ethics in general — if any — would also be valid for information ethics in particular. The forum's participants were particularly careful in simply transferring western ideas to a global information world and were also very concerned that the unification influence of the global Internet can lead to an unwanted dominant general and ethical culture. This is clearly to be seen on (ethical) topics such as property right, violence in the media, information access and information equity, individual freedom of information, where Western philosophical, political, and economic traditions dominate.

Information ethics is not a matter of abstract academic (philosophical) discussion and cannot result in a new (single) world order of information behaviour, but can be a permanent world-wide process of exchange of positions between people who are involved in structuring the new information world. The global information society is thus a platform for information ethics and the result of the discussion cannot be a single world information ethics but the development of an ethos that makes the public aware and sensitive of the need to take a responsible and not only merely economically determined approach towards information, its production, distribution and usage.

This is the major information ethic topic in the information society. The topic is in its global character comparable to ecological questions and should thus be treated on the same level of political decision-making and public disussion. There is a real need for an international information agenda. What VF-INFOethics thus recommends is the development of a world-wide public responsibilty for information equity (an information ethos) by establishing an institutionalized dialog on information policy issues at a world level, 'some authors hold that a new UN/UNESCO information agency would be an approriate institutional means - and by supporting an open world forum (or many interlinked forums) on information ethics, using the electronic medium and other media as well.

Both an institutionalized and a communicative approach will create global (and local!) information policies and information cultures. This means that one should give up the ideal of a rational, clean and transparent ethical world information order, and see the multi-cultural reality not as a threat but as an opportunity.

The continuing globalization of all aspects of the production, distribution and usage of information is the central challenge for information ethics. The production of information is based on the need for information and refers to its content and quality. The distribution of information raises the question of information ownership and depends on the information resources in which information is represented and on the design and management of information market places where information can be accessed and exchanged.

The usage of information is mainly a question of competence and money — being informationally educated in order to profit from the information resources and being able to pay for the costs of information usage. This is a (political) question of information equity or inequity or how to overcome information gaps.

Considering the importance of the global information society, it has turned out that the participants were mainly concerned about the growing gap between those who are able and willing to take advantage of modern information and communication technology and those who are not. The problem of information gaps cannot be restricted to the difference between developed and developing countries but is a problem in all societies, whatever their technological status. If access to information and the possibility to actively take part in the exchange of knowledge (to have the right to read and write in open information environments) is the necessary basis for all activities in our public and private life, then it is UNESCO's responsibility to support all activities which aim at establishing an information balance in the information society.

A society is information-balanced when information gaps can be overcome. Therefore a consideration of information equity seems to be at the center of all ethical discussion. This is not a technological problem. It cannot be solved by providing everyone in the world with a computer and telecommunication equipment (although the importance of such a programme — to provide in principle everyone with the technological basis needed — should not be underestimated), but by solving the information problem.

The forum's participants agreed that only a free market can develop powerful information market places, information systems and information goods but that there is a need for international organizations such as UNESCO and for other nation-wide activities to solve the global problem of information inequity. Overcoming information inequity does not necessarily mean that global information can be accessed from everywhere by everyone (and at no cost). The creation of content in an appropriate environment and the exchange of information among those who need it (for instance, the south communicating with the south and not being restricted to access of information from the north, as is the case today) is increasingly important.

Appendix

eEurope 2005: Information Society for All

The *e*Europe action plan focusing on: "the widespread availability and use of broadband networks throughout the Union by 2005 and the development of Internet protocol IPv6 and the security of networks and information, *e*Government, *e*Learning, *e*Health and *e*Business". The *e*Europe 2002 action plan endorsed by the Feira European Council in June 2000. *e*Europe 2002 is part of the Lisbon strategy to make the European Union the most competitive and dynamic knowledge-based economy with improved employment and social cohesion by 2010. It was complemented by the *e*Europe+ initiative launched by the candidate countries in reply to the invitation of the European Council to take on board the Lisbon strategy. Many of the objectives of *e*Europe 2002 have already been achieved and the remainder will largely be completed by the end of this year. To create a knowledge economy, *e*Europe 2002 focused on extending Internet connectivity in Europe. In order to generate growth, connectivity needs to be translated into economic activities.

Progress During eEurope 2002

— Internet penetration in homes has doubled

— Telecom framework in place

— Internet access prices have fallen

— Almost all companies and schools are connected

— Europe now has world's fastest research backbone network

— e-commerce legal framework largely in place

— More government services available online

— A smartcard infrastructure is emerging

— Web accessibility guidelines adopted and recommended in Member States.

This is the focus of *e*Europe 2005: stimulating services, applications and content that create new markets and reduce costs and eventually increase productivity throughout the economy. Developing content, services and applications and rolling out the underlying infrastructure is predominantly up to the market. Therefore, the action plan will concentrate on those areas where public policy can provide an added value and contribute to creating a positive environment for private investment. Fast progress in digital technologies and the decline in prices for information technology equipment provided business and consumers with more powerful devices. Investment in digital equipment grew throughout the 80s and 90s but when computers became interconnected as the World Wide Web took off in the mid 90s there was a particular boost to productivity. The contribution of the Internet to productivity and growth, particularly in Europe, is therefore relatively recent and much more can be expected. Two new developments will have a major impact on the further development of the Internet: multi-platform access/convergence and broadband.

New communication platforms beyond PC-based Internet access are now becoming available. In particular, interactive digital television and third generation (3G) mobile systems driven by common standards open up possibilities for multiple platform access to services. They can be both substitutes and complements. The same holds for the supporting networks. The Barcelona European Council stressed the importance of open platforms for convergence. Broadband connections significantly increase the speed of transmission between computers, mobile phones, TV set-top boxes and other digital devices. This will improve quality of Internet access, making it more user-friendly and convenient for consumers, and enable the full scope of multi-media applications to be applied.

The next generation of services will rely on these features. If fully exploited, broadband technologies will improve the effective use of networks, and thereby increase productivity and employment. Having any time, anywhere access to information will contribute to greater effectiveness. However, achieving productivity gains through effective use can only be realised by restructuring of economic behaviour to exploit the new technologies: adapting business processes, bringing public services online, enhancing skills.

Realising the potential of broadband requires that everyone is given the ability and opportunity to enjoy and exploit its richness and benefits (in terms of health care, education, and business for example). This means that the goal of the *e*Europe 2002 action plan of achieving an 'information society for all remains valid for *e*Europe 2005. By supporting the emergence of alternative access platforms, such as digital television or 3G mobile systems, the new action plan will further facilitate e-inclusion, also for people with special needs.

The more networks and computers become an essential part of business and daily life, the more security becomes a necessity. Because of the value of current and expected transactions carried out online, networks and information systems need to be secure. Security has therefore become a key enabler for *e*-businesses and a pre-requisite for privacy. The internationalisation of Internet management will also be a key parameter for the harmonious development of the Internet, and the EU will continue to work actively towards this aim.

Broadband enabled communication, in combination with convergence, will bring social as well as economic benefits. It will contribute to *e*-inclusion, cohesion and cultural diversity. It offers the potential to improve and simplify the life of all Europeans and to change the way people interact, not just at work, but also with friends, family, community, and institutions and the way companies operate. This is what users are interested in, and this is where *e*Europe 2005 starts from. The objective of this Action Plan is to stimulate secure services, applications and content based on a widely available broadband infrastructure. The *e*Europe 2002 action plan proved to be a successful format and the basis for similar actions not only in the candidate countries (*e*Europe+), but also in third countries. Its method of

i) speeding up the adoption of new legal measures,

ii) re-focusing existing support programmes, and

iii) defining clear targets to be achieved, combined with benchmarking, had a major impact.

The new action plan will build on these successes and maintain *e*Europe as the symbol of European Union policy to develop the information society. However it needs to be adapted with regard to three requirements.

1. Broadband technology is transforming the Internet and opening up new possibilities for interactive multimedia services only possible at very fast transmission speeds. Infrastructure investment is driven by availability of content and services and the development of new services and content depends on infrastructure deployment. The infrastructure evolves and upgrades when new services and applications emerge and vice versa. *e*Europe 2005 will try to stimulate a positive feedback between infrastructure upgrading, both broadband and multi-platform and service developments.

2. Many measures at European, national and regional level in support of the knowledge economy are already underway. Most Member States have national action plans for information society policy, many of which were inspired by *e*Europe 2002. The *e*Europe 2005 actions should therefore go beyond current policies and make a real difference. They must also be in line with the Barcelona conclusions and take account of the discussions at the Informal Telecom Council in Vitoria.

3. Before the end of this action plan, it is likely that a number of candidate countries for accession to the

EU will be members. It will be a challenge for them (and for the current Member States) to meet the targets and to implement the actions contained in *e*Europe 2005. *e*Europe 2005 therefore needs built-in flexibility and should provide for a midterm review of actions to ensure a smooth phasing in of the new members in the action plan.

The *e*Europe action plan is based on two groups of actions which reinforce each other and build a virtuous circle. The first one concerns services, applications and content, covering both online public services and e-business, and the second one concerns the underlying broadband infrastructure and security matters. The targets of *e*Europe 2005 can be summarised as follows:

By 2005, Europe should have:

— modern online public services

—e-government
—e-learning services
—e-health services

— a dynamic e-business environment and, as an enabler for these

— widespread availability of broadband access at competitive prices

— a secure information infrastructure The action plan is structured around four lines which are interlinked:

– Policy measures to review and adapt legislation at national and European level, to strengthen competition and interoperability, to create awareness, and to demonstrate political leadership.

— the implementation of policy measures is supported by the development, analysis and dissemination of good practices. Projects will be launched to accelerate the roll-out of leading edge applications and infrastructure.

— policy measures will be monitored and better focussed by benchmarking of the progress made in achieving the objectives and of the policies in support of the objectives.

— an overall co-ordination of existing policies will bring out synergies between proposed actions. A steering group will provide a better overview of policy developments and ensure a good information exchange between national and European policy makers and the private sector.

The Actions

Policy measures

Modern online public services

i) e-government

Under the *e*Europe 2002 Action Plan, Member States agreed to provide all basic services online by end 2002. Much has been achieved in this area but many services still have limited interactivity. The Commission and the Belgian Presidency held an e-government conference in November 2001 to identify and disseminate examples of good practice. The ministers participating in the conference adopted a declaration stressing the need to further develop the exchange of good practices and to ensure inclusion and security in online public service delivery.

The development of secure and seamless access to e-government services depends on deployment and the effective use of electronic authentication means. The action taken in support of smart card take-up will continue and could effectively serve this purpose by also providing a secure device to support electronic signature. Improved access to public web sites for disabled people is an objective of *e*Europe 2002. In October 2001, the Council adopted a resolution on e-inclusion and a further resolution in March 2002 stating that Member States should speed up their efforts in implementing the 'Web Accessibility Initiative' guidelines. Access to government services can be facilitated by providing multilingual content and making it available on various platforms. Initiatives regarding e-government exist at national, regional and local level.

These are complemented by actions carried out at European level: the IDA programme is supporting interoperability of back office processes, standardisation and the provision of pan-European services and the IST programme is financing research activities. In addition, the Commission is preparing an initiative to follow up the Communication on creating a EU framework for the exploitation of public sector information. At the Barcelona European Council, Heads of State and Government decided on the creation of a 'one stop European Job Mobility Information Web Site'. This and the portal of the EU administration developed in the framework of the IDA Programme will offer multi-lingual point of access for online information and services to citizens and enterprises supporting mobility across borders. The IDA portal will also serve as test bed for multi-platform technologies. In this context, the use and improvement of machine translation systems to fully cover the linguistic diversity of European users of such web sites will be of importance. The Barcelona European Council also invited the Commission to analyse the role that electronic authentication systems can play in removing obstacles to the development of e-government.

ii) e-learning

Member States responded positively to the ambitious *e*Europe 2002 targets. Most schools are now connected and work is underway to provide convenient access to the Internet and multimedia resources for schools, teachers and students. In Barcelona, the European Council set the target of ensuring by end 2003 a ratio of pupils per on-line computer for educational purposes in EU schools. Trans-European networks connecting national research and education networks have been upgraded substantially but, as yet, few schools are connected.

The Commission has contributed to financing some of these actions through the IST Programme, the eLearning initiative and other actions co-ordinated under the eLearning Action Plan. EU measures included support to the provision of equipment, co-operation and exchange of good practices, teacher training, pedagogical research, and the development of e-learning content and services.

iii) e-health

The work of medical practitioners at all levels is becoming more information intensive as sophisticated medical equipment and computer applications are more widely used. At the same time, demands on healthcare budgets are increasing in the face of medical and scientific advances, an ageing population and changing patient expectations. Digital technologies are becoming more important in health management both at individual practitioner level and at national and regional level. They offer the potential to reduce administrative costs, to deliver health care services at a distance, to avoid unnecessary duplicate examinations.

In addition, the Internet is increasingly used by citizens to obtain medical information. Against this background, it is critical that e-health content and services are developed efficiently, are available for all and health related web sites comply with established quality criteria. More than 10 years of research and development in health telematics and in the framework of the IST programme have been undertaken.

Examples of results are integrated regional health information networks, standardised electronic health records, reliable and effective telemedicine services (teleconsultation and home telemonitoring) as well as personal systems for citizens to support and manage their health status. Another important action already underway which will be contributing to *e*Europe 2005 is to improve the use of telematics in the community pharmaceutical regulatory system (e.g. Eudravigilance for safety of medicines, Europharm Database or e-submission for information exchange between regulatory authorities and industry) which is expected to deliver first results by end 2003.

*e*Europe offers the possibility to combine efforts into a strategy to deliver visible results at the end of the action plan. Health data is particularly sensitive, and all actions in this area must be accompanied by the development of the technical and organisational means to ensure the protection of individuals' health information from unauthorised access, disclosure, and manipulation.

e-business Environment

e-business comprises both e-commerce (buying and selling online) and restructuring of business processes to make best use of digital technologies. Since the publication of the ecommerce communication in 1997, the Commission has developed a comprehensive policy in this field. Among the achievements have been the rapid adoption by the EU of a series of directives, which are aimed at establishing an Internal Market for information society services, as well as a number of non-legislative initiatives aimed at promoting self-regulation, notably in the field of "e-confidence" and online dispute resolution (ODR), and the launch of the 'Go Digital' initiative to help small and medium-sized enterprises to better use e-business. In addition, the tax environment of e-commerce has been adapted and simplified, mainly through the adoption of a directive on electronic invoicing as well as a directive and a regulation on VAT on digital supplies.

The Commission has also launched a debate on the future of consumer policy, regulation and its enforcement. It highlights the need to eliminate regulatory distinctions between the on and off-line world and for future regulation to be created in such a way that it neither becomes redundant or stifles innovation and new technology.

Building on the European Competitiveness Report and on the Communication on the e-economy, the Commission is working in co-operation with Member States to support e-business in Europe. The goal is to promote take-up of e-business with the aim of increasing the competitiveness of European enterprises and raising productivity and growth through investment in information and communication technologies, human resources (notably e-skills) and new business models, whilst ensuring privacy. *e*Europe 2005 will be instrumental in making this policy work.

Information Infrastructure

The European Union has already launched a comprehensive strategy based on the Communications on network security, cyber crime, and the current and forthcoming data protection directive regarding electronic communications. The suggested approach was endorsed and further developed by the Council Resolution of 28 January 2002 and by the recent Commission proposal for a Council Framework Decision on attacks against information systems.

Based on the 28 January Resolution, a number of initiatives (e.g. the establishment of a cyber security task force, awareness campaigns, promotion of good practices, and improved exchange of information mechanisms) should be completed by the end of 2002. This will provide the basis for the work towards a secure information infrastructure. Work on the creation of a secure European smart card infrastructure should continue and the roll-out of applications be intensified. Community research activity on security will continue under the Sixth Framework Programme. Priorities will be: trustworthy network and information infrastructures with an emphasis on emerging technologies (e.g. broadband, wireless architectures, ambient intelligence); the identification of vulnerabilities and inter-dependencies in infrastructures. It also intends to support standardisation with a view to wider use of open standards and open source software. Research activities should also take into account the 'human factor' in security, e.g. basic security standards, user-friendliness of systems.

Broadband

Governments world-wide are increasingly realising that broadband access will be central to the economic development of their countries. Wide availability of broadband communication would have a significant impact on the economy, and several EU Member States have started reviewing broadband development on their territory. Their common objective is to accelerate its deployment. The importance of 'widespread availability and use of broadband networks throughout the Union by 2005' has been recognised by the Barcelona European Council. The actions proposed in this Action Plan correspond to this priority.

Investment in broadband will mainly come from the private sector. In its broad economic policy guidelines, the Commission recommended that "Member States should: ... ensure effective competition in local telecommunication networks (the 'local loop') in order to speed up the development of the European broadband network". Competition is expected to drive investment, generate innovation and lower prices. Therefore, public policy should focus on issues where competition is not effective or where political objectives, e.g. territorial coverage with a view to cohesion, need to be ensured. The new regulatory framework, which will be applied in all Member States from July 2003, takes full account of the convergent nature of broadband. Encouraging efficient investment in infrastructure (by new entrants and incumbent operators) and promoting innovation are explicit objectives for regulators.

This means taking account of the need for investors to obtain an adequate return on their investment, in the light of the risks taken. This also means that regulatory uncertainty for investors must be reduced as much as possible. In the wider context of the European Research Area project, the Commission is supporting the full exploitation of broadband networks by the research community. This will continue under the Sixth Framework Program using the new priority instruments of Networks of Excellence and Integrated Projects.

In specific terms, it will support the upgrade and efficiency of technology for optical fibre access networks, mobile broadband wireless services (beyond 3G), broadband access satellite systems (also taking into account the needs of the Galileo system), convergence of fixed and mobile networks, including the transition to the next generation Internet Protocol (IPv6) and take account of security and privacy issues (wireless, always-on) etc.

The Commission has already set out the steps needed to support the next generation Internet in its IPv6 Communication, "Next Generation Internet - priorities for action in migrating to the new Internet protocol IPv6" and those recommendations should be followed up. A broadband strategy will have a complex task as it is affected by many different policies: town and country planning, research policy, taxation and regulation. They are carried out at all levels: international, European, national, regional and local, and by a range of different actors, private sector as well as public sector.

The Commission will deepen the analysis of policy options and existing obstacles to broadband deployment, in particular with a view to widespread access to new services through open platforms in digital television and 3G, in line with the request from the Barcelona European Council.

Dissemination of Practices

In all areas of *e*Europe 2005, commercial and public applications are being developed, support programmes are running, and experimental applications are being tested. These activities are a rich source of knowledge and expertise. Progress is rapid but uneven, for example one administration or school may be trying to develop or use an application already working somewhere else or for which there is a viable private sector solution. *e*Europe 2005 aims to build upon these experiences. It will not only identify and exploit good practices, but further advance them to act as a showcase which will be instrumental to the achievement of the *e*Europe targets. Good practice activity will therefore be complementary to the policy actions. A three-step approach is proposed:

i. Examples of good practice will be identified, and selected.

The Commission, in close co-operation with Member States, candidate countries, and the private sector, will identify examples of good practice world-wide. This would include practical working examples from the public sector and commercial applications in the areas of the action plan.

ii. Where appropriate, selected good practices will be enhanced to broaden their applicability and an analysis will be carried out to produce a template or guidelines for good practices.

Relevant examples would be extended in scope (e.g. multi-platform instead of single platform or additional users) or complemented by additional developments (e.g. greater functionality or multi-lingual interaction). The demonstration and evaluation aspects of these projects will be reinforced, so that a thorough analysis of the results may be undertaken. The detailed analysis of good practice should result in templates or guidelines.

These provide proven, well-documented approaches to tried and tested applications for e-services. They would be modular and customisable for any particular user and would typically consist of a methodology, an associated set of tools and software in open-source form. This would result in a critical assessment of success factors and lessons of failure, which may lead to transfer and dissemination of good practice across Europe, particularly in the less favoured regions.

iii. The good practices and the results of the project analysis will be disseminated. For the dissemination of good practices, the Commission in co-operation with the Council Presidencies will organise promotional campaigns covering the EU and candidate countries.

This will be based on the following mechanisms:

— Conferences/workshops: The e-government conference with its exhibition of good practice examples is one successful model for an exchange of experience and lessons learnt. An e-health conference which will follow this model is planned for the first half of 2003, as is an e-learning conference and a second e-government conference is proposed for the Italian Presidency.

These conferences normally address policy-makers. They will be accompanied by special dedicated workshops which would bring together the actors for the respective strategies. These events will address in detail the good-practice showcases, templates and guidelines.

— Support networks: Results will be disseminated using existing business, academic, research and user networks - e.g. the e-business support networks to the SME's or the European School Net- and other such channels at the European, national or regional levels. Comparable networks will be sought for actors in all *e*Europe areas. The new Innovative Actions programmes within the framework of the European Regional Development Fund (ERDF) offer regions (in particular, less favoured regions and areas under reconversion) the possibility to test innovative tools and to exchange good practices in regional e-services. This will contribute positively to regional development strategies and thus play an important role within the *e*Europe 2005 action plan.

— A web site: Links to the good-practice templates and guidelines will be published on a specific web site which will provide tools supporting their use and feedback mechanisms.

Benchmarking

Benchmarking of *e*Europe is a 3-stage process.

Definition of indicators

For *e*Europe 2002, indicators were used. The rationale behind these indicators is to focus on output, i.e. the final objective of policy, not the policy itself (e.g. % household connected to the Internet rather than any measure of local loop unbundling). The objective of benchmarking is policy development and this means it is essential to obtain political endorsement of the indicators.

Indicators will need to be updated for *e*Europe 2005 to reflect the revised political objectives. From 2004 onwards, i.e. after the end of *e*Europe+, the new indicator list will also serve as a basis in the Candidate Countries. Where appropriate, regional indicators will be developed.

Measurement and analysis

Internet related statistics soon become outdated and, to retain policy relevance, indicator measurements must be available quickly. Inevitably there is a trade-off between speed and quality. To improve the quality, measurement of *e*Europe 2005 indicators should make greater use of official statistics from the National Statistical Institutes and Eurostat. To allow for regular and comparable data collection in Member States, a legal base is needed for information society statistics.

The Commission will propose this legal base before end 2002. Analysis of the factors underlying indicator values is a key element in exploiting the data for policy development. To enable Member States to undertake their own analysis the results are regularly updated on the *e*Europe web site.

The Commission and the Member States will encourage the development of regional benchmarking, especially with less developed regions in relation to the development of national and regional information society strategies.

Policy development

The value of benchmarking to policy development is evidenced by the Commission's Spring Report to the European Council and the Benchmarking report which provided impetus for the *e*Europe 2005 Action Plan. Benchmarking can be further exploited by exchanging policy good practices. To facilitate this, the Commission will analyse the benchmarking results to identify policy good practices, including regional policies of those Member States, or other countries, with best results in terms of the indicators.

A C-ordination Mechanism for E-policies

Over the recent years many policy initiatives have been launched either as a direct response to the e-economy or to build in an e-dimension into existing policies. Examples at European level are policies such as regional (e.g. support for *e*Europe in structural funds), development (e.g. dotforce - the G8 initiative), education (e.g. e-learning), employment and inclusion (e.g. employment guidelines), trade (e.g. e-commerce in WTO) and the *e*Europe+ action plan. At national level equally, many policy initiatives related to the e-economy have been taken. It is not always guaranteed that the various national measures are well communicated at European level. A better overview and an exchange of information between the various actors would enhance the efficiency of e-policies. For this reason, an *e*Europe steering group, chaired by the Commission (composed of Member States and candidate countries representatives, the European Parliament, and, where necessary, representatives of the private sector and of consumer groups, and funded by the follow-up to the PROMISE programme), should be established. This steering group would monitor progress of the *e*Europe action plan with the aim of improving the implementation of *e*Europe 2005. It would also provide a forum to exchange experiences. It would allow to bring in the private sector and make an early participation of candidate countries possible. The group would in general meet twice a year and with executive level participants to allow a strategic discussion.

Financing

The action plan sets ambitious objectives and proposes actions that will need significant resources. This will be met by using and, where necessary, re-focussing existing programmes. To finance projects and actions at European level, the Commission will make full use of the eTEN and the IDA programmes. Both programmes are currently being re-orientated to support *e*Europe objectives. In particular the financial regulation with respect to the eTEN programme would need to be adapted to make this programme an appropriate tool. The Commission will, where possible, also use available funds of the eContent programme, the follow-up programme of PROMISE , the multiannual programme for enterprise and entrepreneurship, as well as the standardisation, the Internal Market and the industrial competitiveness budget lines. The forthcoming eLearning Programme will also support *e*Europe related activities. The use of funds from these programmes will be in accordance with their legal base.

IST financed projects have been directly relevant to the *e*Europe 2002 action plan and the new IST priority in the Sixth Framework Programme intends to continue to finance research and demonstration projects covering these fields, thus contributing (mostly in an indirect way) to the *e*Europe objectives. This action plan is a proposal to Member States to take some far-reaching commitments. It is an invitation to the private sector to work with the Commission and Member States to realise the *e*Europe objectives. It sets out the initiatives the Commission will or is willing to take. Overall the action plan sets the scene for a co-ordinated European policy approach on information society issues.

The *e*Europe action plan has been confirmed as a key element in the Lisbon strategy. If successful, this plan will have a significant impact on growth and productivity, employment and social cohesion in Europe. One lesson learnt from *e*Europe 2002 is that it would be useful to review actions during the course of the action plan. Therefore a mid-term review, which would coincide with the proposed interim benchmarking report, presented in advance of the 2004 Spring European Council is suggested. The European Council in Sevilla is expected to endorse an Action Plan and invite Council and Parliament to adopt as quickly as possible the necessary legal and budgetary instruments to implement it.

Bibliography

Daniel, Evelyn, 'Information resources and organisational structure', *Journal of the American Society for Information Science*, 1983.

Davis Ruth M., "Computers and Electronics for Individual Services", *Science*, February 12, 1982.

Dray James and Joseph A. Menosky, "Computers and a New World Order", *Technology Review*, May-June 1983.

Franken, H., *et al.*, *Information Technology and the Law,* Lelystad (Netherlands): Koninklijke Verrmande, 1991.

Lane, Elizabeth S. and Summerhill, Craig A., *An Internet primer for information professionals: a basic guide to networking technology*, Westport, Meckler, 1993.

Lloyd Andrew, "Europe Examines Electronic Democracy", New Scientist, June 2, 1983. On Council of Europe report, *New Possibilities for Democratic Participation Resulting From Information and Communication Technology*, Brussels, 1983.

Lynn, M.S., 'Digital Preservation and Access', *Collection Management* 22, nos. 3/4/1998.

Maciuszko, Kathleen, 'A quiet revolution: community online system', *Online*, Nov. 1990, 24-32.

Malamud, Carl, *Exploring the Internet: a technical travelogue*, London, Prentice-Hall, 1992.

Marks, Robert 'The Economic Challenges of Publishing Electronic Journals', *Serials Review* 21, Spring 1995.

McMillan, G., 'Technical Processing of Electronic Journals', *Library Resources and Technical Services* 36, October 1992.

Parag Diwan & Shammi Kapoor, 'Cyber & E-Commerce Laws, Bharat Publishing House, 2000.

Parsons, G. L. 'Information technology: a new competitive weapon', *Sloan Management Review,* Autumn 1983.

Simons G. L., *Privacy in the Computer Age* NCC, Manchester, England, 1982.

Rahul Mathan, 'The law relating to computers and Internet', Butterworths India, 2000.

The Spreading Danger of Computer Crime, *Business Week,* April 20, 1981.

Weizenbaum Joseph, *Computer Power and Human Reason: From Judgement to Calculation* W. H. Freeman, San Francisco, 1976 and Penguin, Harmondsworth, England, 1984.

Whisler, Thomas, *The Impact of Computer on Organisation,* Praeger, 1970.

Wood Michael, *Introducing Computer Insecurity* NCC, Manchester, England and John Wiley, New York, 1983.

Index

Adequate infrastructure, 6
Archiving systems, 135

Budgetary constraints, 134
Business process outsourcing (BPO), 68
Business-to-business (B2B), 63
Business-to-consumer (B2C), 64

CD-Recordable (CDR), 160
Cisco Networking Academy Program (CNAP), 77
Competitive advantage, nature of, 5
Compound Annual Growth Rate (CAGR), 86
Confederation of Indian Industries (CII), 68
Copyright laws, 156
Critical Enabling Skills Training (CREST), 19
Customer Support Service (CSS), 100

Development paradigm, 14
Digital books, 141
Digital economy, 8
Digital Millennium Copyright Act (DMCA), 158
Disseminate information, 127
Distance learning applications, 16

E-book formats, 146
E-businesses, 263
E-commerce practitioner, 63
E-commerce, segments of, 66
Economic dimensions, 129
Education, promotion of, 15
E-journals, 137
Electronic data processing (EDP), 87
Electronic publishing, 127
Employment stability, 9
Equipment, provision of, 268
European Regional Development Fund (ERDF), 276
Europharm Database, 269

Foreign exchange earnings, 11
Formal financial sector, 84
Fundamental shift, 71

General policy environment, 99
Geographical Information Systems (GIS), 69
Global export markets, 11
Gross Domestic Product (GDP), 155

Hypertext Mark-up Language (HTML), 130

Information and Communication Technologies (ICT), 1
Information technology equipment, 261
Information, symmetry of, 23
Infrastructure deployment, 264
Institution-based work, 69
Interactive digital television, 262
International Coalition of Library Consortia (ICOLC), 165
International Data Corporation (IDC), 67
International Intellectual Property Alliance (IIPA), 155
International Telecommunication Union (ITU), 60
Internet Protocol, 273

Knowledge economy, 260

Labour, global division of, 3
Least Developed Countries (LDCs), 130

Macro-policies, 4

Management practices, 2
Mass communication, origin of, 127
Minimal educational requirements, 81
Mobile pay phone services, 65
Multi-media applications, 262
Multiple-choice questions, 92

Networking technologies, 66

Office Equipment (OE), 87
Online Dispute Resolution (ODR), 270
Online Service Provider (OSP), 159
Organizational changes, 5
Organizational hierarchy, 10
Outsourcing operations, 67

Peer review, 139
Peer-to-peer technology (P2P), 153
Physical disabilities, 20
Print On Demand (POD), 142

Qualitative change, 5

Rapid technological change, 2
Regulatory framework, 272

Skill polarization, 2
Skills, polarization of, 18
Small and Medium-sized Enterprises (SMEs), 65
Software development, 76

Telecommunications, 12
Telephony services, 65
Time-consuming investments, 13
Trade-Related Aspects of Intellectual Property (TRIPS), 154
Traditional microenterprises, 80

Union Network International (UNI), 21

Value-added production, 13
Very Small Aperture Terminal (VSAT), 78

Wireless architectures, 271
World Telecommunication Development Report (WTDR), 78
World Wide Web (WWW), 130